Bill Clinton

Titles in the United States Presidents *series:*

United States Presidents

Bill Clinton

Michael A. Schuman

Series Consultant:
Don M. Coerver, professor of history
Texas Christian University, Fort Worth, Texas

Enslow Publishers, Inc.
40 Industrial Road   PO Box 38
Box 398   Aldershot
Berkeley Heights, NJ 07922   Hants GU12 6BP
USA   UK
http://www.enslow.com

Acknowledgments

Many thanks to the following people who took time from their busy schedules to talk with me and add their insights to this book and/or assist me in other ways: Leon Panetta, Carolyn Staley, David Leopoulos, Joe Purvis, Elaine Johnson, Rose Crane, Tom Caplan, Tom Campbell, Dave Matter, Paul Root, Cora McHenry, Mary Anne Salmon, and Michael Moore. And thank you once more to the staffs at the Keene, New Hampshire Public Library and the library at Keene State College.

Copyright © 1999 by Michael A. Schuman

Library of Congress Cataloging-in-Publication Data

Schuman, Michael
    Bill Clinton / Michael A. Schuman
      p. cm. — (United States presidents)
    Includes bibliographical references and index.
    Summary: Describes Bill Clinton's rise to the presidency as well as the ups and downs he experienced during his two terms in office.
    ISBN 0-7660-1036-8
    1. Clinton, Bill, 1946– —Juvenile literature. 2. Presidents—United States—Biography—Juvenile literature. 3. United States—Politics and government—1993– —Juvenile literature. [1. Clinton, Bill, 1946– . 2. Presidents. 3. United States—Politics and government—1993–] I. Title. II. Series.
    E886.S38   1999
    973.929'092—dc21
    [B]   98-53046
                                              CIP
                                              AC

Printed in the United States of America

10 9 8 7 6 5 4 3 2

To Our Readers: All Internet addresses in this book were active and appropriate when we went to press. Any comments or suggestions can be sent by e-mail to Comments@enslow.com or to the address on the back cover.

Illustration Credits: AP/Wide World Photos, p. 73; *Arkansas Democrat-Gazette*, pp. 36, 41, 45, 48, 51, 64, 81, 86; Arkansas Post Card Company, p. 18; C.N.P./Archive Photos, pp. 21, 66; © Corel Corporation, p. 27; Ed Cromwell, Cromwell Architects and Engineers, p. 15; Ernest Ricketts, p. 35; George Bush Presidential Library, p. 63; Georgetown University, pp. 26, 29; Michael Marsland, Yale University Office of Public Affairs, p. 71; Michael Moore, p. 92; Nasir Hamid, University of Oxford, p. 31; Reuters/Soile Kallio/Archive Photos, p. 102; Rose Crane, pp. 14, 16, 46; United States Department of State, p. 98.

Source Document Credits: CNN Website, p. 108; Georgetown University, p. 10; Joseph H. Purvis, p. 17; National Education Association, p. 52; Rose Crane, p. 6; TOLES ©1998 *The Buffalo News*. Reprinted with permission of UNIVERSAL PRESS SYNDICATE. All rights reserved, p. 114.

Cover Illustration: Courtesy of the White House.

Contents

STATE OF THE UNION

ADDRESS TO THE 106th CONGRESS

FIRST SESSION

President William J. Clinton

JANUARY 19, 1999 • WASHINGTON, D.C.

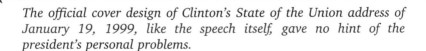

The official cover design of Clinton's State of the Union address of January 19, 1999, like the speech itself, gave no hint of the president's personal problems.

1

A STRANGE DAY
IN HISTORY

President Bill Clinton stood before both houses of Congress on the evening of January 19, 1999. Millions were at home that evening, watching on television as the president delivered his State of the Union address, an annual speech every president gives in January. Its purpose is to allow the president of the United States to brief the citizens on the state, or condition, of the nation. On this evening, Clinton was well into his second term as president.

Clinton told the nation,

> Because of the hard work and high purpose of the American people, these are good times for America. We have more than 14 million new jobs, the lowest unemployment in twenty-four years, the lowest core inflation in thirty years, incomes are rising, and we have the highest home ownership in history. Crime has dropped for a record five years in a row, and the welfare

rolls are at their lowest in twenty-seven years. Our leadership in the world is unrivaled. Ladies and gentlemen, the state of our union is strong.[1]

The facts proved Clinton was right. The murder rate in the United States was the lowest it had been in thirty years.[2] The economy had grown steadily for seven years, and businesses were making more money than ever before. America was enjoying its longest peacetime economic boom since the end of World War II.[3] The fact that the United States was not at war with any nation only seemed to reinforce the point that Americans were indeed enjoying good times.

The vast majority of citizens agreed. Over the course of the previous year, public opinion polls showed that between 63 and 71 percent of the American people approved of Clinton's performance as president.[4] Those are unusually high ratings for any national leader.

Despite this extremely rosy picture, something was drastically wrong in the United States of America. Just a few short hours before the president gave his State of the Union address, a trial officially began in the United States Senate. Its purpose was to judge whether the president of the United States was still fit to do his job.

Almost from the beginning of Clinton's first term as president, an ongoing investigation had been conducted into a business transaction he had participated in years earlier. In 1978, Clinton and his wife, Hillary, had invested money in a planned Arkansas resort named Whitewater, along with another couple, James and Susan McDougal. The resort went bankrupt, and the investors, including the Clintons, lost money.

When Clinton became president in 1993, rumors

circulated that the first couple had committed illegal acts to lessen their financial losses from this real estate project. For example, the Clintons were accused of not paying their income taxes fairly. At different times, two independent prosecutors, or unbiased lawyers hired to find the truth in a legal case, were assigned to look into the Whitewater matter. Neither prosecutor ever found the Clintons guilty of any wrongdoing regarding Whitewater.

Then, in 1994, a second problem arose for the president. A woman named Paula Jones claimed publicly that Clinton had sexually harassed her. Just twenty years ago, sexual harassment did not exist as a legal issue. However, the problem was gradually brought into the public's consciousness by the National Organization for Women (NOW) and other feminist groups. There are many different actions that constitute sexual harassment. Jones accused Clinton of making an unwanted sexual advance toward her in a hotel in 1991.

Clinton denied doing anything wrong. He admitted he may have met Jones briefly, but he stated that nothing illegal or inappropriate had happened.

During Clinton's second term, the second special prosecutor, Kenneth Starr, began turning his attention from Whitewater to other alleged illegal activities committed by Clinton. The fact that these activities had no apparent relationship to the Whitewater matter bothered many people. It seemed as if Starr, a conservative Republican, was simply on a witch-hunt, a mission to discredit or ruin the president, who was the first Democrat in the White House since Jimmy Carter left office in 1981. Many feared that Starr was not really looking for justice, but was just trying to find some way to hurt Clinton

The signature of Bill Clinton, the forty-second president.

politically. Still, Starr had been given official permission by Clinton's attorney general, Janet Reno, to take his investigation into different directions.

Then, in January 1998, it seemed Starr finally found what he was looking for. Clinton was accused of having an extramarital affair with a young White House intern named Monica Lewinsky. When questioned under oath about his relationship with Lewinsky, Clinton denied having a sexual relationship with her. However, over the course of the year's ongoing investigation, facts were released that made it clear that Clinton did indeed have a physical relationship with the intern. The president was accused of lying under oath, a very serious charge. Clinton explained that although he did have a physical relationship with Lewinsky, it was not sexual. Some critics thought the president was just playing with words and manipulating the truth. Clinton was also accused of obstructing justice, or interfering with a legal investigation, another severe claim. He flatly denied any obstruction of justice on either his part or that of any of his staff members.

Because of these two legal charges, Clinton was impeached, or accused of "high crimes and misdemeanors," by the United States House of Representatives in December 1998. Impeachment is the official charge of serious wrongdoing that can lead to removal from office.

As a result of the impeachment charges brought against him, Clinton would have to face trial in the United States Senate. If two thirds of the senators found him guilty of either charge, he would be removed from office.

It was just hours before Clinton delivered his State of the Union address when the United States Senate began its solemn impeachment trial. Clinton mentioned nothing about these proceedings in his speech. Although he was fighting for his life, politically speaking, the president appeared as if everything was business as usual in the nation's capital.

Opinion polls taken earlier that month showed that a full two thirds of the American people did not want Clinton to be removed from office, and that less than one third were even paying close attention to the impeachment proceedings.[5] Part of this polled majority may not have approved of the president's personal actions, but they did not think they were severe enough to warrant removing him from office. Other parts did not feel the president's personal life was the public's business. Still others believed Clinton did lie under oath, but that independent prosecutor Starr's tactics were even worse than Clinton's actions.

Regardless of one's personal view, one fact was clear: January 19, 1999, was one of the most unusual days in American political history.

2

A PLACE CALLED HOPE

T he story of Bill Clinton's life really begins three months before he was born. It starts in Hope, Arkansas, a small farming town located in the southwestern part of the state, thirty miles from the Texas border. Until Clinton became a candidate, the town was best known for producing some of the largest water-melons in the nation.

Clinton's parents, William and Virginia Blythe, were living with Virginia's parents in their boxy, two-story house with six rooms, located not far from some railroad tracks. The Blythes did not plan to stay there long. William had recently been discharged from the Army after fighting in World War II. He had just found a job as a traveling salesman for a heavy equipment company. However, the job was based in Chicago, and the Blythes would have to move from Hope.

Since the new home they were building was not ready, Virginia decided to stay in Hope with her parents. She was pregnant with the couple's first child. William Blythe spent the winter of 1946 living in a hotel in Chicago.

By the spring, their new house was finished. William drove south to Arkansas with plans to bring Virginia to Chicago. The couple looked forward to many happy years in their new home.

On May 17, 1946, Virginia received a telephone call that changed her life. She was told that her husband had been killed in an automobile accident in Missouri.

Instead of moving to Chicago, Virginia decided to stay in Hope to live with her parents, Edith and Eldridge Cassidy. Three months later, Virginia gave birth to a son at Julia Chester County Hospital. The date was August 19, 1946. The baby was named William Jefferson Blythe III, in memory of his father.

At that time it was traditional for married women to stay home to raise children while their husbands worked to support the family. However, with her husband dead, Virginia would have to support herself and her new son. First she would have to learn a trade. When her baby was about a year old, Virginia moved to New Orleans to train as a nurse anesthetist.

For most of the next two years, young Billy was raised by his grandparents, the Cassidys. Often the toddler was found in their kitchen studying playing cards pinned to the curtains. His grandmother had placed them there so Billy would learn numbers.

Virginia returned to Hope in 1949 and began work at a local hospital. She and her son continued to live with the Cassidys. Billy's grandfather, Eldridge, owned a grocery

When he was a baby, Bill Clinton stayed in Hope with his grandparents while his mother trained in New Orleans to be a nurse anesthetist.

store on North Hazel Street in Hope. It was on the outskirts of a mostly African-American section of town, known as Colored Town. (The term *African American* was unheard of then. Black persons were called *colored* or what was at the time a more respectful term, *Negroes*.)

Segregation, or the deliberate separation of the races, was legal in most of the South. African Americans were forced by law to remain apart from whites in many public places such as movie theaters, restaurants, buses, and trains. There were separate schools for both races. Even bathrooms and drinking fountains were segregated into "white" and "colored" sections.

Segregation was based on the attitude that blacks were inferior to whites. The term commonly used for that belief is *white supremacy*. Legally, facilities for African Americans and whites were supposed to be separate but equal. However, they were almost never equal. Most schools, businesses, and other facilities for African Americans were inferior to those for whites.

Eldridge Cassidy was unusual among business owners in the South in the 1940s. He believed it was fine to allow both whites and African Americans to shop in his store. He was also known as a generous man who freely let customers buy on credit, which meant they could pay at a later date when they had more money.

Joe Purvis, a friend of Bill Clinton's since childhood, recalled that Cassidy made a huge impression on the future president: "Bill spent a lot of time with his granddaddy at his store. I'm convinced that's how he became aware of the situation of blacks and black life under segregation in the 1940s and 1950s. It made a deep and vivid impression that stayed with him the rest of his life."[1]

Joe Purvis and Billy Blythe attended a private kindergarten together. Purvis remembered that they liked to dress up and play cowboys. He recalled how he and Billy enjoyed going to see cowboy movies on Saturday afternoons at a local theater. For a combined total of ten cents, they got to see two movies along with a cartoon and an episode of a serial, or continuing feature.

This watercolor rendering of Clinton's first home in Hope, Arkansas, was painted by architect Ed Cromwell.

Billy Blythe loved reading. He enjoyed Little Golden Books and the works of Beatrix Potter, author of the Peter Rabbit series. He was also known in his neighborhood as a peacemaker who often tried to stop fights between other children.

One regular customer at Cassidy's grocery store was a divorced man named Roger Clinton. He ran a Buick dealership in Hope. Billy's mother, Virginia, got to know him through his visits at her father's store. Virginia soon fell in love with him, and they married on June 19, 1950. Billy was almost four years old. Virginia and Roger moved into a new home a short distance from Virginia's parents. It was a one-story house on South Thirteenth Street in a neighborhood bursting with young families.

Billy's mother, now Virginia Clinton, had no idea that her new husband harbored several dark secrets. He had problems with both alcohol and gambling, and he had regularly beaten his first wife.[2] Soon after marrying Virginia, Roger Clinton began to physically and mentally abuse her, too.

Early in 1953, when Billy was in the second grade, Roger Clinton decided to move to the town of Hot Springs, Arkansas, where he had grown up.

Billy Blythe was nearly four years old when his mother, Virginia, remarried. Her new husband was Roger Clinton, a car dealer.

SOURCE DOCUMENT

THE WHITE HOUSE
WASHINGTON

January 29, 1999

Joseph H. Purvis
Dover & Dixon
425 West Capitol Avenue
Suite 3700
Little Rock, Arkansas   72201

Dear Joe:

Thank you for your recent letter. It's always good to hear from you, and I was really happy to see you over the holidays.

I understand your concern about the dedication of the Birthplace in Hope. I plan to be there on March 12, barring any unforeseen problems. I'll look forward to visiting with you then.

Sincerely,

Clinton still keeps in touch with his childhood friend Joe Purvis. This letter from Clinton refers to the official dedication of his birthplace in Hope, which took place on March 12, 1999.

He sold his Buick dealership and moved his family to Hot Springs, about sixty miles northeast of Hope.

Hot Springs and Hope are different types of towns. Hot Springs is a flashy resort. Tourists come to relax in its thermal waters. There is a horse-racing track, and in the past, gambling casinos operated illegally there. Famous entertainers came regularly to perform in the casinos.

Roger Clinton went to work at a Buick dealership in

Hot Springs. Virginia became a nurse anesthetist at a local hospital. Even though Billy had not been officially adopted by Roger, the small boy began calling himself Bill Clinton. He also called Roger "Daddy," in spite of the fact that his stepfather did not spend much time with him.

Although the Clintons were Baptists, Virginia enrolled Billy in a Catholic school for the rest of second and third grade. It was smaller than the public schools, and she thought it might make the transition to the new town easier. For fourth grade, Virginia transferred her son to the public Ramble Elementary School.

Billy made the adjustment to the new school well. One of his best friends was David Leopoulos, who said, "When I first met him we were in the schoolyard, I remember him

A composite photo of Clinton's first-grade class shows the future president in the top row, second from the left.

coming up to me and saying, 'Hi. I'm Bill Clinton. What's your name?' At that age I was kind of taken aback. It was unusual for a child to act like that."[3]

In 1956, Roger and Virginia Clinton had another child, a boy they named Roger, Jr. Billy, now ten, was very protective of his baby brother.[4] David Leopoulos remembered that he and Billy frequently baby-sat for little Roger and took him with them when they went out.

Bill's stepfather continued to drink and act violently toward Virginia. Most of the time, he did so in private. Bill's friends were not aware he had a troubled home life. Years later David Leopoulos said, "Bill never shared his grief. . . . Sometimes I'd be over his house and I'd say something and wouldn't get an answer. His mind would be off in another area. Maybe he'd be anticipating what might happen that night."[5]

One night when Bill was fourteen, he decided he had had enough. By then he had grown to be six foot one, the same height as his stepfather. Bill heard Roger, Sr., fighting with Virginia and Roger, Jr., in their bedroom. Bill broke down the door and announced he would no longer tolerate any abuse. He told Roger, Sr., "You will never hit either of them again. If you want them, you'll have to go through me."[6]

In time, Virginia decided she, too, had had enough. She filed for a divorce from Roger, which was granted on May 15, 1962. Bill was a fifteen-year-old high school student. However, right after the divorce became final, Roger begged Virginia to take him back. They were remarried just three months later.

Soon afterward, Bill legally changed his last name from Blythe to Clinton. It had been a long time since anyone had referred to him as Bill Blythe, and he hoped that changing his name would be good for family unity.

Clinton was a busy student at Hot Springs High School. He played tenor saxophone in the high school band and was named band major. He was so talented he made the all-state band. Outside of school he played in a jazz trio with two friends.

In many ways, Clinton's teenage years were typical of many young people's in the early 1960s. Weekends consisted of attending high school football games, followed by a visit to Cook's ice-cream store. Sometimes the teenagers attended high school dances at the local YMCA and YWCA.

One group Bill joined was the Boys' Nation, which is run by the American Legion. Its purpose is to teach young people about government and civic leadership. There was also a Girls' Nation. To be elected to either organization by one's classmates was an honor. Both Clinton and his friend Carolyn Staley were selected to attend the combined group's national convention in July 1963 in Washington, D.C. Part of their stay included a tour of the White House. When the young delegates were touring the Rose Garden, they received an unexpected visit from President John F. Kennedy, who came out to meet them. Kennedy shook some of their hands, including Bill Clinton's.

Staley recalled, "When we came back [home] we were on a cloud. Our classmates were enormously proud of us. . . . Three pages of our yearbook were devoted to us. . . . Bill wrote in my yearbook something like, 'Guess we will never forget this, will we?'"[7]

Just four months later, on Friday, November 22, President Kennedy was assassinated in Dallas, Texas. The time was 12:30 in the afternoon. Most Americans were at

In July 1963, President John F. Kennedy paid a surprise visit to the delegates from the Boys' and Girls' Nation. Here, Clinton shakes hands with the president.

work or school. The students at Hot Springs High School learned the tragic news when Principal Johnnie Mae Mackey announced it over the school intercom. A friend named Phil "Jet" Jamison remembered the moment that Clinton heard the news. Jamison said, "He was motionless. Not even a twitch on his face. Yet you could feel the anger building up inside him."[8]

As a high school senior, Bill hoped to run for student

body president. However, Principal Mackey wanted as many students as possible to take part in extracurricular activities. Bill was already band major, so he was not permitted to run for president. Instead, he ran for class secretary. His opponent was his friend Carolyn Staley. She remembered that Clinton joked to her, "If you beat me for this, I'll never forget it."[9] She won the election, but the two have remained good friends ever since.

Politics and music were Clinton's twin passions at this time of his life. He loved debating ideas and current events with his mother and with other students. On most political issues, he sided with the Democrats.

His friend David Leopoulos maintained, "In the classroom he was impassioned and with his mother he was impassioned, and he would never back down. Many times he and his mother disagreed, and you'd see the veins showing in his face, just like I saw the other day when he was on television."[10]

Hot Springs High School held graduation ceremonies for its senior class on May 29, 1964. When the final rankings by grades were figured, out of a class of three hundred sixty-three seniors, Clinton ranked fourth.[11]

3

DOMINOES AND LOTTERIES

In the fall of 1964, Clinton traveled east to Washington, D.C., to attend Georgetown University. The future president was attracted by Georgetown's School of the Foreign Service.

The years he spent at Georgetown—1964 to 1968—were among the most eventful years in the twentieth century. Many people today think of the 1960s as a decade of hippies, student radicals, and political disorder. The main reason for these drastic changes was the Vietnam War.

The little country of Vietnam is located in southeast Asia. At the time, Vietnam was divided into two countries. North Vietnam was Communist. South Vietnam was not.

In pure communism, all businesses are owned collectively by the community, and there is no private enterprise. However, the communism practiced in Asian countries such as China and North Vietnam is not pure communism. All businesses are owned by the government instead of the community. The only official political party is the Communist party, and there is little tolerance for people with different views. Citizens who openly criticize their governments are often punished.

North and South Vietnam were fighting what was essentially a civil war. Some Americans feared that North Vietnam would overtake South Vietnam and make it a Communist country, too. These Americans believed in the Domino Theory—that if one nation were taken over by Communists, then all the nations in that region would follow and topple like dominoes.

The United States had had military advisers in South Vietnam since the 1950s. However, in 1965 Lyndon Johnson was the first president to send combat troops to Vietnam to play an active role in the war.

By 1967 the war seemed endless. Young American men were dying by the hundreds every week in that tropical foreign land. Many Americans were starting to question the United States' role in the war. They wondered whether North Vietnam was really trying to spread communism or simply trying to unify the country. If the latter theory were true, should young American men be risking their lives in what was basically a foreign civil war that had no effect on the security of the United States?

Although Americans of all ages openly opposed the war, those who took part in active protests were mostly young. Their viewpoint had a special urgency: They would be the ones who would be called upon to fight.

In protesting the Vietnam War, many young people began to reject their parents' values. In their minds, their parents' rigid thinking had helped bring on this questionable involvement in a foreign war. Many young people examined their parents' other values, too, and made it a point to act and look as different as possible from the establishment, or the powerful people in business and government. Men burned their draft cards in public, although it is an illegal act, and those who were caught went to jail. Most did so willingly, proud of their strong stand against the United States' actions abroad.

Although Bill Clinton entered college in 1964, his behavior—and that of most of his fellow students—was of a 1950s mindset. Georgetown was a conservative college. Clinton's roommate, Tom Campbell, recalled that when it came to trends and activism, Georgetown was "two or three years behind most other colleges."[1] Campbell explained that male students had to wear jackets and ties to classes, that no girls were allowed in men's dormitories, and that strict curfews were enforced.[2]

In college, Clinton continued to be as active as he had been in high school. He ran for president of the freshman class and won. One of his favorite professors was Carroll Quigley, of the Department of Civilization. Clinton always remembered what Quigley said in one lecture: "The thing that got you into this classroom today is belief in the future, belief that the future can be better than the present, and that people will and should sacrifice in the present to get to that better future."[3] Outside the classroom, Clinton kept busy, too. He took part-time jobs to help pay for his education. Socially, he had many friends and dates. His first girlfriend at college was a tall, quiet young woman from New Jersey named Denise Hyland. Their first date was dinner at an Italian restaurant, and before long they were seen everywhere together.

Clinton (left) was soon active in college politics, becoming president of his freshman class at Georgetown. With him are Judith Baiocchi, secretary; David Kammer, vice-president; and Paul Maloy, treasurer.

Clinton was elected class president again in his sophomore year. Denise helped by passing out literature and organizing groups of supporters. The following summer, Bill went home to Arkansas to work on his first political campaign. A judge named Frank Holt was running for the Democratic nomination for governor of Arkansas. Holt ultimately lost the nomination, but by working for him, Clinton made valuable political contacts, including the staff of Arkansas senator William Fulbright. Fulbright was head of the Senate Foreign Relations Committee and one of the first congresspersons to oppose the war publicly.

When he returned to Washington that fall, Clinton was hired as a clerk in Fulbright's office. Because he worked long hours there, Clinton decided not to run for student office during his junior year at Georgetown.

Part of Clinton's job was to gather the names of Vietnam War casualties who had come from Arkansas and give them to Fulbright. Clinton's college friend Tom Campbell remembered, "Seeing those casualty lists coming in all the time, he was personally aware of the impact the war was having on people's lives. He saw how many kids the war was killing."[4] Like millions of other Americans, Bill Clinton was now convinced that the Vietnam War was wrong.

The names of Arkansans killed in battle, which Clinton gathered for Senator William Fulbright, now appear on the Vietnam War Memorial in Washington, D.C., along with the names of all the other soldiers lost in the war.

As his junior year was nearing an end, Clinton decided to run for president of the entire Georgetown University student body. The term would be served during his senior year. Clinton's opponent, Terry Modglin, ran as an outsider (a candidate who was not part of the political system). That tactic helped him beat Clinton by a total of 717 to 570 votes.[5]

That summer, Clinton was given a special opportunity. Senator Fulbright had encouraged him to apply for a Rhodes Scholarship, a prestigious fully paid grant. It would enable young people to study at Oxford University in England. Only the most brilliant and capable students receive Rhodes Scholarships. Clinton became only the second student from Georgetown University to win one.[6]

Clinton's campaign manager, Dave Matter, remarked, "Bill told me that if he had been elected student body president he probably would not have had the time or the inclination to try for a Rhodes Scholarship. He told me it was a blessing in disguise. Whether it was true or not, I don't know. But it made me feel better."[7]

Despite losing the election, Clinton was no less popular. His girlfriends included a brainy blonde named Ann Markesun, and the reigning Miss Arkansas, Sharon Ann Evans. He was never at a loss for male friends, either. It was clear he liked people and they liked him.

Clinton's senior year covered a tragic time, both in his personal life and in the outside world. In November 1967 his stepfather died of cancer. Although stepfather and stepson had never gotten along well, losing a family member to cancer is never easy. Then, on the evening of April 4, 1968, Dr. Martin Luther King, Jr., was assassinated in Memphis. Clinton was deeply saddened. He was a strong supporter of the civil rights movement and a great admirer of its leader.[8]

Angry African Americans took to the streets and rioted in cities across the country. One of the hardest hit was Washington, D.C. Clinton's friend Carolyn Staley happened to be flying into Washington for a visit. She and Clinton volunteered to help riot victims.

Clinton graduated from Georgetown University in 1968. This is his yearbook picture. In the fall, he traveled to Oxford University in England on a prestigious Rhodes Scholarship.

She remembered, "It was very clear to me that Bill Clinton was not content to sit on the sidelines or to stay on campus. Because he felt he was called to someday be a public servant, he wanted to do what his heroes in public service would do—that is get involved and take action."[9]

In the fall of 1968, Clinton was off to Oxford, England. He enjoyed Oxford, and found the work not as hard as he had imagined. He played rugby in his spare time and still managed to read three hundred books his first year.[10]

One aspect of English life disturbed Clinton, however. He said, "I ate lunch in the market almost every day, and I spent a lot of time talking to ordinary citizens, not just university people. I was always struck by the distinctions of class . . . something I thought was not a good thing."[11]

While he was in England, Vietnam and the draft were always on Clinton's mind. He organized public forums on issues relating to the war. He knew it was just a matter of time before he would have to face the draft himself.

For years, all college students had been protected from the draft. The result was that young men from poor families who could not afford to go to college were the ones likely to be drafted, and they did most of the fighting. The system seemed to represent exactly what Clinton disliked most about distinctions of class. President Lyndon Johnson agreed. So in 1968 Johnson abolished the draft exemption for graduate students. Once a student earned a bachelor's degree, he was eligible for the draft.

The United States government began a lottery system that would decide who would be drafted. Lottery numbers were chosen once a year. Men who were, or were about to turn, nineteen years old were called to report for the draft

Oxford University in Oxford, England, is the oldest British University. It was begun in the twelfth century.

in the order of their draft numbers. Whether a man would go to war was a matter of the luck of the draw.

Like millions of young men, Clinton did not want to fight in the Vietnam War. Many found ways to avoid being drafted. Some had or faked medical conditions that made it unsafe for them to fight on active duty. Others went so far as to fail to report for induction and risked being sent to jail. Some fled to Canada and other foreign countries. Still others enlisted, which gave them the right to choose where they would be stationed. Those who were drafted were told by military authorities where they would have to go, which most likely would be Vietnam.

Another option for college students was a division of the military called Reserve Officer Training Corps (ROTC), an officer-training program offered at most colleges. A man in ROTC would probably not have to fight in Vietnam. At the end of his first year at Oxford, Clinton returned to Arkansas to apply for an ROTC scholarship.

Taking this course of action meant he would not be able to return to Oxford for a second year. (A British college like Oxford would not offer an American ROTC program.) So Clinton planned instead to attend law school at the University of Arkansas, which did have ROTC.

However, in the fall of 1969, Clinton canceled his ROTC agreement and returned to Oxford. He would take his chances with the draft lottery, after all. The number drawn for Clinton was 311. With such a high number, the chances were slim that he would actually be drafted. His worries about Vietnam were over.

Many people have speculated on Clinton's reason for dropping his ROTC commitment. A friend from Oxford named Rick Stearns said Clinton began to feel guilty thinking about earning an officer's commission and a law degree while a poorer man would have to fight in his place. Stearns said that Clinton told him he felt he was "running away" from the duty others were facing.[12]

Clinton's critics have claimed that he was merely a draft-dodger and took a coward's way out. If he had drawn a low draft number, he would still have been able to fall back on his ROTC scholarship. Either way, Clinton was safe at Oxford for one more year.

4

LOVE AND POLITICS

C linton left Oxford after two years. He had been accepted at Yale University Law School in New Haven, Connecticut, for the fall of 1970. Although Clinton had a scholarship, it did not cover all his law school and living expenses, so he took different jobs to help make ends meet. He took a part-time teaching job at the University of New Haven and also worked for a local attorney. As a third job, he aided a city councilman from nearby Hartford.

By this time, the young law student had stopped wearing jackets and ties as he had at Georgetown. Now his appearance was relaxed, to blend in with the youthful and informal fashions of the times. His mother remembered one time when "he was wearing shorts and a T shirt and those big, ugly rope sandals people used to wear back then. His hair was thick and wild and sticking out to there."[1]

In one of Clinton's law classes was a young woman with light brown hair. One afternoon in the law library they kept eyeing each other from separate tables. She finally walked up to where he was sitting and said, "If you're going to keep staring at me and I'm going to keep staring back, we should at least introduce ourselves. I'm Hillary Rodham."[2]

Soon the two were dating regularly.

Hillary Rodham was as ambitious as Bill Clinton. Unlike Clinton, however, Rodham had grown up in a wealthy community—a suburb of Chicago called Park Ridge, Illinois. Her father was a successful businessman, a textile manufacturer, and her mother, like most women of the day, stayed home to care for her family.

Years later Rodham recalled that her family was very different from Clinton's: "I came from a very Republican family that was not particularly fond of the Roosevelts and not particularly fond of the Kennedys. . . . I really did come from a background that was highly suspicious of government and very supportive of the individual and individual responsibility."[3]

She began to depart from her family's views in 1965. Rodham supported Martin Luther King, Jr., and the civil rights movement. She claimed that her turning point was the Voting Rights Act signed by President Johnson in 1965. The act guaranteed the right to vote for all people. Before the act was signed, various southern states had laws making it difficult for African Americans to vote.

Rodham remembered, "From that time on I supported a lot of the goals of the Johnson administration domestically, even though I became very concerned about the Vietnam War and very much opposed it."[4]

*Unlike her future husband, Hillary Rodham (bottom row, far right)
came from a wealthy family and grew up in an affluent community.
This is her sixth-grade class picture.*

Before her graduate years at Yale, Rodham received an
undergraduate degree from Wellesley College, in
Massachusetts, outside Boston. She was elected president
of the student body, and at her college graduation ceremony in 1969, she was the student chosen to speak to her
fellow graduates.

While at Yale, both Clinton and Rodham found time to
be active in politics. In 1970, he ran a campaign office for
a minister and antiwar activist named Joseph Duffey who
was running for, but ultimately lost, a United States Senate
seat from Connecticut.

Two years later, in 1972, both Clinton and Rodham
took breaks from their studies to work for South Dakota
senator George McGovern in his race for president.
McGovern was the Democratic party nominee running

against Republican president Richard Nixon. Like Joseph Duffey, McGovern was a strong antiwar activist.

The law students' work for McGovern meant a brief move from Connecticut to Texas. Clinton became the Texas state coordinator for the campaign, while Rodham helped register voters in San Antonio. The work proved to

At Wellesley College, Hillary Rodham was elected president of the student body. She also spoke at commencement: "The challenge now is to practice politics as the art of making what appears to be impossible, possible. . . ."

be a valuable political experience for Clinton, even though McGovern lost the election in a landslide.

Clinton and Rodham both graduated from Yale Law School in 1973. He was twenty-six years old and eager to return to his beloved Arkansas. Hillary Rodham took a job as an attorney for the Children's Defense Fund, a non-profit group working for children's rights, in Boston. The two promised to stay in touch.

Clinton was planning to open a law office in his hometown of Hot Springs. From there he thought he might run for office. However, his plans changed when a Yale professor told him that the University of Arkansas was looking for new teachers. Although Clinton was only twenty-six years old and seemed too young for the job, Clinton persuaded Wylie Davis, dean of the law school, to hire him to teach law for one year.

So Clinton moved to Fayetteville, home of the University of Arkansas, in the fall of 1973. Fayetteville was very different from the Arkansas towns where Clinton grew up. For one thing, its citizens were mostly Republicans, whereas those of Hope and Hot Springs were mainly Democrats.

While Clinton was settling in as a college teacher, Hillary Rodham was making a major career move. After only six months working for the Children's Defense Fund, she was recruited for a unique opportunity. In Washington, D.C., the House Judiciary Subcommittee was looking into the possibility of bringing articles of impeachment against President Richard Nixon. Rodham was offered a chance to work for the committee.

Impeachment was such a political rarity that until that time only one president—Andrew Johnson—had ever been so disgraced. Rodham could never have imagined that twenty-five years later, and 130 years after Andrew Johnson, her own future husband would be the second president to be impeached.

Nixon was at the forefront of a scandal known as Watergate. It began in June 1972 when five men connected to the Republican party were caught breaking into the Democratic party headquarters, located in a building complex called Watergate on the outskirts of Washington. It was believed that these burglars were trying to steal secret information for Nixon to use against the Democrats in the 1972 presidential campaign. In time, Nixon was accused of trying to block a legal investigation of the crime. That action would be obstruction of justice. If Nixon were impeached and convicted, he would be forced out of office. It was up to the impeachment inquiry staff to find out whether Nixon should be formally accused of any serious crimes concerning the Watergate affair.

In the 1970s, it was unusual for a female lawyer to be taken seriously. Of more than one hundred members of the committee staff hired to look into Nixon's actions, Rodham was one of only three women.[5] She was put to work on uncomplicated legal matters such as serving subpoenas, or written statements ordering a person to appear in court.

On one occasion, Clinton flew into Washington to visit her. Just before his visit, Rodham told a fellow attorney named Bernard Nussbaum that he ought to meet her boyfriend. "He's going to be president of the United States," she bragged.[6]

The impeachment inquiry staff never finished its work.

Nixon resigned the presidency on August 9, 1974, before he could be impeached, or formally accused of a crime.

The Watergate scandal affected many people in office, even some far from Washington. In Arkansas, Republican congressperson John Paul Hammerschmidt had long been a strong defender of Nixon. His congressional district included the heavily Republican town of Fayetteville, and he had never had much trouble being elected. In fact, he had never even faced a serious challenge since he was first elected to the House of Representatives in 1966.

Because of Watergate, however, Nixon supporters were now suffering from guilt by association. Those who had supported Nixon were viewed, rightly or not, as part of a corrupt Washington power structure. If there were ever a year in which a Democrat could beat Hammerschmidt, it was 1974. Bill Clinton asked some Democratic friends to run against Hammerschmidt. When they refused, Clinton decided to do it himself.

Since Rodham's work in Washington was finished, she decided to move to Fayetteville. The move to small-town Arkansas would be a huge adjustment for Rodham, who was used to life in big cities such as Chicago, New Haven, and Washington. Some of her friends thought she was foolish to make the move. One was a young woman named Sarah Ehrman whom she had met while campaigning for George McGovern in Texas. Ehrman remembered repeating to her friend, "You are crazy. You are out of your mind. You're going to this rural, remote place—and wind up married to some country lawyer."[7]

Hillary realized the move would be difficult, but she confessed, "When you love somebody, you just have to go and see what it's like. So I moved to Arkansas and started teaching at the [University of Arkansas] law school."[8]

She also helped run Clinton's congressional campaign. He ran hard, and on election night it looked as if Clinton might actually win. As of midnight, he was leading by several thousand votes. However, the votes from Sebastian County, a Republican stronghold, had not yet been received. When those votes finally came in, the results showed that Hammerschmidt was winning by only six thousand votes.[9] Right away, there were rumors about illegal voting in Sebastian County. Some of Clinton's staff members suggested that he challenge the election results, but he decided it was not worth the trouble.[10] His close fight made news throughout the state. Even though he lost, Bill Clinton made a name for himself as an up-and-coming politician.

Running for office was now in his blood. Clinton knew he would run again in 1976. He considered challenging Hammerschmidt for Congress once more. He also gave thought to the post of Arkansas state attorney general. Beating Hammerschmidt would be tough. It might be easier to be elected attorney general, which would give Clinton real government experience. Critics said his lack of experience had hurt him in the 1974 campaign.

In the summer of 1975, Hillary Rodham took a trip, first to visit friends in Chicago and then to the East Coast. She was in for a surprise when she returned to Fayetteville. Clinton had bought a small stone and brick cottage she once said she liked. He told her it would be hers if she would marry him. She agreed, and they were married in the living room of their new house on October 11, 1975.

Rodham decided that although she was married, she would keep her own last name. That was an unusual custom in 1975, especially in the South, which remained more traditional than the rest of the country.

Within a year of getting married, Clinton was elected state attorney general. He hired his old friend Joe Purvis from Hope to work with him. Purvis became the deputy attorney general in charge of the criminal division. He explained, "Clinton was young, bright, and energetic, and

Bill Clinton and Hillary Rodham were married in Fayetteville, Arkansas, on October 11, 1975, in the living room of their new cottage. Hillary kept her own last name.

he hired young people like him[self] who wanted to make a difference and not just sit there and collect a paycheck."[11]

Clinton's biggest accomplishment as attorney general was reforming the state penitentiary system. Conditions had been so poor, and prisoners were mistreated to such an extent, that Arkansas's prisons had been declared unacceptable, according to the state constitution. Under Clinton's leadership, the prisons were brought up to constitutional standards.

Clinton also received praise for aiding consumers in disputes against the big utility companies, especially the powerful Arkansas Power & Light (AP&L). Purvis remembered that Clinton constantly "looked over the shoulders of the utilities companies. He made sure they could justify their rate hikes. He looked out for the little guy not usually represented in disputes with big utilities companies."[12]

After two years as a successful attorney general, Clinton felt it was time to move on to something bigger. He had set his sights on becoming governor of Arkansas. Clinton's only obstacle was a rumor being circulated that a decade earlier he had dodged the draft. However, the rumor failed to stick, and in November 1978, Clinton was elected. On January 9, 1979, at the age of thirty-two, Bill Clinton was sworn in as the nation's youngest governor in forty years.[13]

5

"AN IQ OF A ZILLION"

C linton went to work as governor with the force of an Arkansas twister. He outlined a new budget for the state. It called for the largest increase in money for public education in the state's history.[1] This funding included large salary increases for teachers. At the time, the state of Arkansas ranked near last in the United States in spending on education.

Clinton also called for a new state Department of Energy. Early in 1979, a massive oil shortage hit the nation. In large part, the shortage was due to a decision by oil-producing nations to cut back on their exports. Some said it also came about because of waste by American consumers: Americans drove big cars that used large amounts of gasoline. Others blamed big American oil companies, whom they accused of purposely causing an oil shortage to force prices upward.

Whatever the reason for it, American leaders tried to find ways to tackle the oil crisis. Governor Clinton thought the answer, at least for Arkansas, was a state Department of Energy. Its purpose would be to conserve and regulate the cost of energy in his state.

That solution did not sit well with Arkansas Power & Light, the giant business that provided utility services to consumers. AP&L had no competition and was not used to being told what to do.

At the same time, Clinton also took on the timber industry. Arkansas is a heavily wooded state where many earn a living in the lumber business. Clinton felt that clearing out so many acres of woodland should be scaled down or the environment would suffer.

Clinton's childhood friend Rose Crane, Arkansas director of the Department of Natural and Cultural Heritage in 1979 and 1980, admitted, "We tried to move too fast, tried to make too many changes too soon."[2]

Another problem Clinton tried to fix was the state's highways. At that time, they were in bad shape. Yet, repairs cost money. Where would the governor get the money to fix the roads?

He could have canceled his plans to increase teachers' salaries, but he felt that education was too important to ignore. The only option was to raise taxes. To accomplish this goal, Clinton supported a plan to raise taxes on car registration tags, gasoline, and tires. His plan was approved by the Arkansas state legislature.

Clinton soon learned that he had misjudged the people of his home state. They were outraged by the increased tax on car registration tags. Some were paying ten times as much as they had before.[3] At the same time, the nation

After he was sworn in as governor in 1979, the nation's youngest in forty years, Clinton went to work on a large number of projects.

was suffering from high inflation, a condition where the cost of goods and services was increasing at a very fast pace. This economic problem was in large part due to the severe oil shortage.

When the governor appeared before the public, he was strongly criticized. Many Arkansans resented not only Clinton's deeds but his staff as well. Most of his advisers were young, and some wore beards. Critics speculated that Arkansans felt uneasy about a staff that seemed too liberal for the state.

There was a break from the bad news on February 27, 1980, when Hillary gave birth to a daughter. The baby was named Chelsea Victoria Clinton after a favorite song called "Chelsea Morning" by folksinger Judy Collins.

The birth of Chelsea, the Clintons' only child, was the extent of the good news for the couple in 1980. Another incident hurt the governor that year. This time, it was not his fault.

The story began in Cuba, a Communist island nation ninety miles south of the Florida Keys in the Caribbean Sea. For years, Cubans seeking to live in a democratic country have tried to leave Cuba. Under Cuban law they are not permitted to do so. Some bravely escaped in small

Despite his busy life as a politician, Clinton still found time to play his saxophone.

boats, but those who did not want to risk their lives in this manner had no choice but to remain on the island.

In 1980, Cuban dictator Fidel Castro decided to let some Cubans emigrate, or leave the country, in the name of human rights. However, his intentions were not entirely noble. Along with willing emigrants, Castro loaded boats leaving Cuba for the United States with prison inmates and patients from mental hospitals. President Jimmy Carter felt it would be inhumane to send the boats immediately back to Cuba. But what would he do with the refugees once they landed in the United States?

Under Carter's direction, the United States government sent them to Fort Chaffee, a military base in Arkansas. There they would be processed, and the government would decide who would stay and who should be sent back.

On May 26, roughly three hundred fifty Cubans broke out of the fort and rioted throughout the towns near the base. Clinton took immediate action. He called officials at the White House and insisted that federal troops at the fort be given permission to use force, if necessary, to stop the rioters. By the next morning, federal troops were given that permission. However, it was Arkansas state troopers and local police who did most of the work returning the Cubans to the fort.

Yet damage was done to Clinton, who was up for re-election in 1980. His Republican opponent was a business executive and former Democrat named Frank White. White tapped in on the voters' frustrations. One of White's political ads on television showed filmed footage of rioting Cubans. The ad blamed Clinton for allowing the refugees to be sent to Arkansas, even though it had been President Carter's decision, not Governor Clinton's. Rose Crane remembered that White ran his campaign against Clinton "based on 'Cubans and car tags.'"[4] The strategy worked. Clinton lost the election, becoming the youngest defeated governor in United States history.[5]

Clinton took a job at a private law firm in Little Rock, but he was anxious to be back in public office. The loss depressed him, and he often secluded himself. Meanwhile, Frank White was turning out to be an unpopular governor. Whereas Arkansas voters thought Clinton may have tried to accomplish too much too soon, they condemned White for being too conservative. Under White, the Arkansas legislature passed a law requiring public schools to teach

Ex-governor Clinton hugs Hillary after his farewell speech in 1981. Clinton became the youngest defeated governor in the history of the United States.

the theory of creationism (the biblical story of Adam and Eve) if they were allowed to teach about evolution. Although a large number of religious Christians live in Arkansas, many were uneasy about teaching the Bible in public school.

Clinton started working on his political comeback. He met with civic groups, and he chatted with local people on his daily morning jogs. He learned that many objected not just to the car tag tax. They also did not like the way he had pushed the car tag law through the legislature without first taking time to learn what the citizens wanted. Clinton quickly learned that not talking with the people was a big mistake. He admitted about himself, "A guy who supposedly has an IQ of a zillion did something stupid."[6]

Elaine Johnson was Clinton's campaign coordinator for Hempstead County, Arkansas, which includes Clinton's birthplace of Hope. She described what happened next: "He called all the people who ran his campaign in 1978. They met at local chambers of commerce in every county. His question to all of us was, 'Do you think I can make a comeback, and if so would you be willing to help us?'"[7]

Johnson continued, "I said I thought he could win again. The people of Arkansas wanted to give him a slap on the hand [for the car tag tax], but did not want him out of office."[8]

On February 27, 1982, the ex-governor once more declared his candidacy for governor. On the same day, his wife publicly referred to herself as Hillary Clinton, instead of Hillary Rodham. Perhaps she hoped that taking her husband's last name would appease conservative Arkansans critical of her progressive attitude.

Clinton campaigned with enthusiasm for reelection.

Elaine Johnson explained, "He is probably one of the best campaigners ever. He can talk to anyone on their basis—in the cornfield, in the chicken houses, in the little country store."[9] In the November 1982 election, Clinton defeated Frank White with 55 percent of the vote.[10]

Right away, he went to work on his main goal: improving the state's public school system. At the time, the average teacher's salary in Arkansas was roughly fourteen thousand dollars per year. Out of the fifty states, Arkansas ranked fiftieth in teachers' pay.[11] Clinton's plans had several parts. He formed a commission to study the system and make suggestions on how to improve it. He appointed his wife to head the commission.

To raise teachers' salaries, it would be necessary to increase the state sales tax one percent. This time the people of Arkansas approved the tax increase. Clinton's Quality Education Act was passed in September 1983.

Why did the people approve this tax increase and not the car tag tax of his previous administration? Paul Root, a special assistant to the governor, explained, "He did a better job of selling it [the tax increase]. He spent three or four nights a week discussing the need for better education at town meetings across the state. He asked people, 'Are you willing to spend more money to improve the quality of education?' Night after night 70 to 80 percent said yes."[12]

Naturally, the teachers' union, the Arkansas Education Association, strongly supported Clinton on this issue. However, they did not support Clinton's order that all teachers take tests to prove they were qualified to do their jobs. Parents had complained that some teachers had misspelled words and used poor grammar when correcting their children's homework. Clinton cited the story of a teacher who did not understand Roman numerals and who referred to World War II as "World War Eleven."

Paul Root explained, "The people of Arkansas said we'll vote for higher taxes if you'll show us some evaluation of teachers. There was tremendous reaction by the teachers to this. They felt they had been betrayed."[13]

One account reported that a total of 25,077 teachers and aides took the first round of tests. According to the report, a total of 1,315 failed.[14] Some reports said that these teachers had to leave their profession to find other work. However, Paul Root said that was not the case:

"The law was written so that a teacher who failed the

Clinton and four-year-old daughter Chelsea enjoy watching a Christmas parade together.

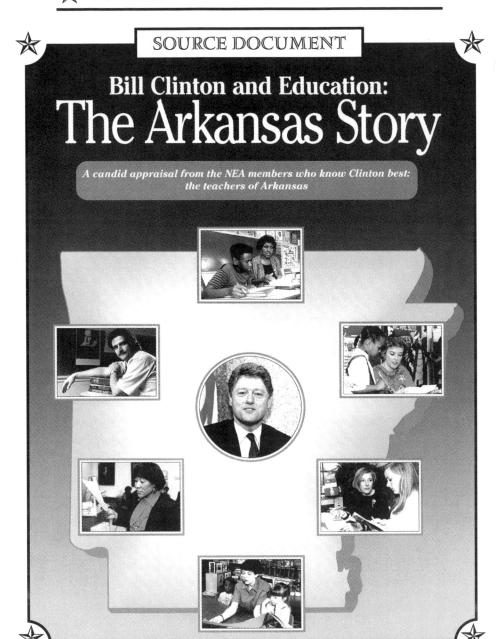

Bill Clinton and Education:
The Arkansas Story

*A candid appraisal from the NEA members who know Clinton best:
the teachers of Arkansas*

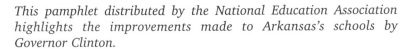

This pamphlet distributed by the National Education Association highlights the improvements made to Arkansas's schools by Governor Clinton.

test would not be recertified. But teachers with bachelors degrees had six years to take the test [again] and pass. Teachers with masters degrees had ten years. There were a lot of early retirements. . . . But no one was fired."[15]

Clinton was becoming known as the education governor and gaining good publicity. At the same time, however, there were personal problems in his family. They had managed to be kept secret, but in 1984, these troubles exploded onto the front pages of the newspapers.

That summer, Clinton's brother, Roger, was arrested for selling cocaine. He pleaded not guilty and was freed on bail. Luckily for the governor, Roger's problems seemed to have little effect on the voters of Arkansas. They reelected Clinton in November with 63 percent of the vote.[16]

As soon as the election was over, Roger changed his plea to guilty. The two brothers and their mother held a family meeting. Roger tried to convince his family that he was not addicted to cocaine, but they knew better. Bill helped place his brother in a drug treatment program. There the family met for group counseling sessions. For the first time, the family talked openly about Roger Senior's addiction to alcohol.[17] The three talked out many of their problems. In February 1985, Roger Clinton was sentenced to two years in prison for dealing cocaine.

Clinton went on to busy himself with his duties as governor, while Hillary worked hard at a private law practice called the Rose Law Firm. Now and then rumors were circulated stating that the Clintons' marriage was not a happy one. It had been reported several times that Clinton had been unfaithful to his wife. None of these accounts were proven. Still, Clinton's enemies gave him a nickname: Slick Willy.

Despite rumors about Clinton's infidelity and Roger's drug problems, most Arkansans were happy with the governor. Besides improving education, his efforts to attract small businesses to move to his state were paying off.

By the mid-1980s the governor of this small southern state was beginning to attract national attention. In 1986, Clinton was elected vice-chairman of the National Governors' Association. He pushed moderate Democratic party ideas. One was called "workfare," an alternative to welfare, which is a government system of giving money to the needy. The money is supplied by the government, which gets it from taxes paid by the citizens. By the mid-1980s, many Americans believed a large number of welfare recipients were getting a free ride. Clinton's "workfare" idea would help welfare recipients find jobs and not be as reliant on the welfare system.

Clinton was easily reelected in 1986. By then, the state had changed the law to give governors a four-year term in place of two years. Political writers and analysts were considering Bill Clinton a possible presidential candidate for 1988. However, on July 15, 1987, he declared in a public speech that he would not run for president. He explained that a presidential run would require him to spend too much time away from seven-year-old Chelsea.

At the 1988 Democratic National Convention in Atlanta, Clinton was asked to give a nominating speech on behalf of Massachusetts governor Michael Dukakis. The exposure could have been a golden opportunity for Clinton. Tens of millions of viewers would be watching the convention on live television. Instead, the evening turned disastrous for Clinton.

The trouble started when nobody turned down the

lights in the hall. Dim lights would have signaled the crowd to quiet down and make Clinton the center of attention. In addition, every time Clinton mentioned Dukakis's name, fans called out, "We want Mike." The interruptions spoiled Clinton's rhythm and caused his speech to drag on. ABC, one network covering the convention, cut off Clinton's speech as it passed the twenty-one minute mark. After thirty-two minutes, when he finally said, "In conclusion," the audience cheered.

For the next few days, Clinton was the butt of jokes across the country. Comedian Johnny Carson quipped that Clinton had been approved by the surgeon general as an over-the-counter sleep aid.

Clinton was then invited to appear on *The Tonight Show*, hosted by Carson. He took Carson up on the offer. Rather than make excuses, Clinton poked fun at himself and his speech. He offered to make a similar speech for George Bush, Dukakis's Republican opponent, in order to make Dukakis look good.

"He laughed at himself and the people liked that," said Mary Anne Salmon, a Clinton staff member.[18]

Because of his positive attitude, Clinton emerged from the 1988 campaign with a better image than Dukakis. The Republican party's presidential nominee, George Bush, then Ronald Reagan's vice-president, ran a negative and misleading campaign. Dukakis never fought back, and Bush, a household name, clobbered Dukakis in the general election.

Clinton ran for governor again in 1990 and won easily, but he seriously set his sights on bigger things in 1992.

6

"HE DOESN'T QUIT."

M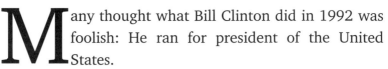any thought what Bill Clinton did in 1992 was foolish: He ran for president of the United States.

Sitting president George Bush was running for re-election. Early in 1991, Bush had led the United States to victory over the nation of Iraq in a six-week military conflict known as the Persian Gulf War. Iraq had invaded and occupied its neighbor in the Middle East, the small country of Kuwait, situated on the Persian Gulf. Kuwait supplied oil to the United States, and Americans were concerned that Kuwait's oil exports would be cut. That would probably mean a return to gas shortages like those of the 1970s, or worse.

Because of the United States' superior performance in the Gulf War, Bush's approval rating was as high as any president's had been in decades. Well-known Democrats assumed that Bush, a Republican, would be reelected with ease. No Democratic candidate who had run for president in 1988 tried opposing Bush in 1992.

When Arkansas governor Bill Clinton entered the Democratic party race on October 3, 1991, there were only a few declared Democratic candidates. None, including Clinton, had a name familiar to voters. Arkansas county coordinator and Clinton friend Elaine Johnson said, "We all thought in 1992 that Clinton was running for name recognition. We thought that with Bush's [high] ratings he [Clinton] would not be elected, but would be well known when he ran in 1996. We never dreamed he would be elected in 1992."[1]

As 1992 progressed, something unexpected began to happen. The nation's economy was turning sour. Unemployment and inflation were rising. Many Americans were concerned about losing their jobs and businesses.

President Bush declared that in time the economy would fix itself. Still, most Americans blamed Bush for the poor economy. By July 1992, his approval rating had nosedived to 30 percent.[2]

Aside from criticizing Bush, Clinton offered solutions to the country's economic problems. He promised a tax cut for the middle class, the largest majority of voters and perhaps the group most burdened by taxes. Polls showed that Americans were concerned about the rising cost of health care, from routine doctor appointments to life-saving surgery. Clinton promised that affordable health care would be one of his top priorities.

In addition, Clinton shied away from traditional Democratic party solutions. The Democrats were regarded as the party of big and expensive government-sponsored social programs. Republicans had won the last three presidential elections with calls for smaller, less expensive government, mocking the Democrats' "tax and spend" policies. Clinton stated that he supported smaller government and less government spending than his fellow Democrats. Yet he did not want to remove government programs that were vital. To sum up his position, he referred to himself as a "new Democrat."

To be elected president, Clinton first had to be chosen, or nominated, by his party. In every state each party holds either a primary election or a meeting called a caucus to choose its favorite nominee. In most cases, the person who is selected by the most states becomes the party's nominee, or candidate.

Every four years, the first presidential primary election takes place in New Hampshire. In 1992, it was slated for February. Throughout much of January, Clinton led the other Democratic contenders. Then a bombshell was dropped. Clinton had continued to be dogged by rumors that he had been unfaithful to his wife. In January 1992 a supermarket tabloid newspaper named the *Star* printed a story about a woman named Gennifer Flowers who claimed to have had an extramarital affair with Clinton for twelve years.

The majority of articles in tabloids such as the *Star* are not taken seriously. These publications are known for printing rumors and outright lies. In addition, it soon became known that the *Star* had paid Flowers thousands of dollars for her story. Because of that payoff, many people did not trust the truth of Flowers's story. However, because her claim involved a person trying to become the leader of the free world, the legitimate media followed up the *Star*'s report. They wanted to know the truth about Flowers's accusation. Reporters asked Clinton repeatedly for his response to her claim.

Finally, Clinton decided he must speak directly to the people. He and Hillary appeared together on the television news magazine program *60 Minutes* directly following the 1992 Super Bowl. Clinton denied Flowers's claim that he had had a twelve-year-long affair with her. Clinton was also asked if he was ever unfaithful to his wife. Without directly saying yes or no, he admitted that he "had caused pain in my marriage."[3] Most viewers believed he was answering yes.

Yet the majority of Americans refrained from judging Clinton solely on that issue. The fact that the Clintons had appeared on the television program together impressed some viewers that their marriage was strong, if not ideal. Some Americans understood that very few people could live up to such intense personal scrutiny, and they refused to judge another person's private matters. They were more concerned with public issues, like whether Clinton could heal the sick economy.

Barely had the Flowers incident been addressed, when another Clinton scandal arose. Once again, the issue of his draft status in 1969 was questioned. To some military veterans, Clinton seemed a cowardly draft-dodger. However, those who had opposed the Vietnam War did not fault him.

In some ways Clinton was his own worst enemy. He never gave a definite answer to reporters about how he had managed to avoid being drafted. Through their research, journalists saw that over the years Clinton had given answers that contradicted each other.

Because Clinton seemed so reluctant to be straightforward, some reporters became eager to catch him in a lie. On one occasion he was asked if he had ever smoked marijuana. He answered that yes, he had tried marijuana years earlier, but had never inhaled. Because that comment seemed too phony to be true, it became a joke across America. That statement also became symbolic of what some saw as Clinton's talent for manipulating words to avoid damaging truths.

Clinton's friend David Leopoulos was one of the few who said he believed Clinton's remark about not inhaling: "He's not a smoker. Smoke gagged him. I almost wish he wasn't so honest. I knew no one would believe him. I think he should have said, 'I tried it and I didn't like it.' But he gave an honest answer."[4]

Nevertheless, what appeared to many people to be a lack of honesty cost Clinton public support. His popularity dropped sharply in the polls. Journalists said he was finished. Leopoulos said it was time to fight back. He drove three days from Little Rock to New Hampshire to help his friend's campaign. Leopoulos recalled,

> We had gone from 30 percent in the lead to 30 percent behind. Then I addressed several campaign workers. I told them how I grew up with Bill and what a decent man he was. Everyone sort of perked up and said that maybe this guy is worth fighting for. [5]

Clinton finished second in the New Hampshire primary. Former Massachusetts senator Paul Tsongas received 36 percent of the vote. Clinton earned 25 percent.[6] The Clinton staff was pleased with those figures. Tsongas was from a state that borders New Hampshire and was better known in the region. Also, Clinton had managed an amazing comeback when many had counted him out.

Clinton continued to do well throughout the nation's primaries and caucuses, and he won enough delegates to earn his party's nomination. Yet soon he faced a second challenge. Billionaire Texas businessman H. Ross Perot entered the race as an independent candidate. Because he was not a professional politician, Perot appealed to many people. The presence of Perot caused concern for supporters of both Bush and Clinton. A third-party candidate like Perot had little chance of winning the general election. Yet he could draw enough votes away from Bush or Clinton to hurt either candidate.

By mid-July, Perot was still a power to be reckoned with. Americans appeared to want an alternative to Bush and Clinton. To many, Bush was unable to handle his job, as the downturn in the economy had shown. Yet Clinton did not seem totally honest. To these skeptics, Perot was the answer, that is, until he dropped out of the race on July 16. The independent candidate claimed his family was being hurt by personal attacks.

Clinton then concentrated his campaign on criticizing Bush's record. As summer turned into fall, the nation was still suffering from an economic slump. By then, Clinton was passing Bush in the polls.

At the Democratic National Convention in New York City, Clinton chose Tennessee senator Al Gore as his running mate. Putting a Tennessee resident on the ticket with Clinton was a strategy the Democrats hoped would attract Southern voters. The South had voted almost solidly Republican since the 1960s. Like Clinton, Gore was a political moderate. He promoted both environmental issues and the need for bringing the "information superhighway," or the Internet, to citizens and schoolchildren across the country. In addition, his wife, Tipper, had spearheaded a campaign to place parental guidance labels on rock music albums deemed unsuitable for children. Conservative Republicans had long attacked the Democrats for being weak on traditional family values. This time, with the Gores on their ticket, the Democrats knew such criticisms would have a hard time sticking.

There was one more important factor in Clinton's choice. Both Gore and Clinton were in their forties. George Bush was in his sixties. His predecessor, Ronald Reagan, was nearly seventy when he was elected president in 1980. Now, the Democrats would appear to be a young and vibrant party.

Perot surprised the nation by reentering the presidential race in early October, and the contest was back to three contenders. In a way, Perot's indecisive behavior made Clinton appear strong. Unlike Perot, Clinton never allowed personal attacks to force him to quit. Clinton's mother, Virginia, who had survived both cancer and an abusive husband, said of her son, "He doesn't quit. I should know. I taught him that."[7]

The three candidates faced off in three televised debates. Perot charmed viewers with his down-home sense of humor. Clinton held his own. In one debate, Bush implied that Clinton had been unpatriotic by not serving in the military and by opposing the Vietnam War.

Despite the old question of Clinton's patriotism, Clinton had heavy support from one sizable segment of the population: women. He was openly in favor of keeping abortion legal. Bush was not. In addition, Clinton had

In the 1992 presidential race, Clinton squared off against Republican George Bush (left), the current president, and third-party candidate H. Ross Perot (center) in a series of televised debates.

clearly chosen and proudly supported a wife who fit the modern image of a strong, independent woman, and he seemed to understand issues that concerned working women. While conservative women disagreed with the Clintons' public policies and nontraditional family roles, liberal and moderate women were attracted to them.

When the votes were counted on Election Day, Clinton had clobbered Bush in the electoral college, 370 to 186 votes.[8] Some called it a landslide. But was it really?

Of the popular vote, Clinton received 43 percent. Bush picked up 37 percent and Perot 19 percent.[9] Republicans were quick to point out that although Clinton had won the election, well over half the American public had voted against him. Democrats countered that his victory had been more difficult than usual because there had been three candidates in the race, instead of the usual two. In the end, the exact figures mattered little: Bill Clinton had definitively been elected the forty-second president of the United States.

On election night, Clinton gives his victory speech from the Old State House in Little Rock, Arkansas.

7

A ROUGH START

I naugeration week 1993 was a landmark event filled with parties, balls, and concerts. William Jefferson Clinton was the first president born after World War II. For the first time, a presidential inaugural celebration included music from rock, blues, pop, and hip-hop acts such as Blues Traveler, Linda Ronstadt, Little Feat, and Salt-N-Pepa. The inaugural theme song was a rock classic: "Don't Stop (Thinking About Tomorrow)" by the legendary band Fleetwood Mac.

Clinton started thinking about tomorrow as early as his inaugural speech on January 20. He said, "To renew America we must be bold. We must do what no generation has had to do before. We must invest more in our own people, in their jobs, and in their future, and at the same time cut our massive debt."[1]

No celebration lasts forever. Just after the president's inaugural speech, veteran news correspondent Charles Kuralt told fellow journalist Dan Rather, "We are pretty hard on our presidents . . . and this one may as well know we're going to be hard on him, too. . . . You can bet though he's only forty-six today, he'll be fifty-six in about a year."[2] Truer words were never spoken. Clinton barely had time to get his feet wet before he was bombarded with criticism. One of his first acts as president was to fulfill a campaign promise to end a ban on homosexuals in the military. He called such a ban a form of discrimination.

However, that act quickly blew up in Clinton's face. The military establishment was not used to being challenged about its traditional ways of conducting business. It was not about to take an order that threatened age-old

Rap star M.C. Hammer stands between Tipper and Vice-President Al Gore at one of the inaugural balls.

practices, especially not from a president who had not even served in the Vietnam War.

In addition, homosexuality is an emotionally charged issue. Whereas many consider it a harmless alternative lifestyle, others consider homosexuality a sin against nature. Those who supported allowing homosexuals in the military felt that the group had been unfair victims of discrimination, just as African Americans had been earlier in our nation's history. Persons against homosexuals in the military felt it would destroy a unit's ability to bond, which in turn could hurt the unit's ability to fight effectively. Those without strong feelings either way were annoyed that Clinton was making this issue a priority while the national economy was suffering. A "don't ask, don't tell" compromise finally settled the matter. It was decided that if homosexuals kept their lifestyles to themselves, they would not be forced to leave the military.

Almost immediately, Clinton reneged on his campaign promise to deliver a tax cut for the middle class. He confessed he had no idea how deep the federal deficit really was until he became president. Proposing a tax cut would only add to the national debt and hurt the economy more.

Statistics showed that the federal deficit was indeed $20 billion higher than Clinton believed it to be at the time of his election. At its current rate of growth, the national debt would be more than $400 billion by the year 2000.[3] Still, some believed Clinton never had any intention of offering a tax cut. They felt he had made a false promise just to be elected more easily.

Clinton went on to propose a tax increase that would affect mostly the middle class. It was a small tax on heating fuels, and it was passed by Congress as part of a larger budget bill. However, most tax increases Clinton proposed would affect only the wealthiest Americans. He also planned some increases in government spending. The majority of these funds were aimed at programs for the future. The increases included more money for job training and education reform. He wanted funds to help existing government programs such as Head Start, and the Women, Infants, and Children Act (WIC). These programs improve the basic health and education of children from poor families. Most of these projects were included in a bill referred to as the Stimulus Bill. However, Clinton did a poor job of convincing Congress to support it, and the bill was defeated early in 1993.

Clinton did keep his promise to tackle the health care system. In an unusual move, he appointed his wife to head a commission that would develop a plan to reform health care. No first lady since Eleanor Roosevelt had played such a powerful public role in the workings of government. It was both Clintons' hope that no persons would ever be denied medical treatment because they were poor.

Meanwhile, the Clintons did their best to keep Chelsea, now twelve years old, out of the public eye. She attended a private school, and most members of the media respected the president's and first lady's wishes to grant Chelsea her privacy.

Clinton was in office barely three months when far away from Washington a bizarre incident occurred. It would have an explosive impact on the Clinton administration and on all Americans. A religious cult named the Branch Davidians was living in a communal compound near Waco, Texas. Their leader was a man named Vernon Howell, who had changed his name to David Koresh. He was wanted by the federal government for breaking laws regarding illegal possession of firearms. There were reliable reports that Koresh was abusing women and children inside his compound.

On February 28, 1993, federal agents tried to arrest Koresh. The cult members were well armed and began shooting at the agents. When the battle was over, four agents had been killed, and sixteen others had been wounded.[4] After the gun battle, a siege of the compound by federal agents began. They surrounded the compound and waited, hoping those inside would surrender. The siege lasted fifty-one days, until April 19. On that day, federal agents in armored vehicles charged the Branch-Davidian compound. Rather than surrender, cult members committed mass suicide by setting their entire compound on fire. A total of eighty-six Branch Davidians, including several children, died.[5]

Although Clinton accepted "full responsibility" for the failed assault, he implied that the deaths were really the fault of cult leader David Koresh.[6] The vast majority of Americans agreed, although some ultraconservatives blamed the government for unlawfully "invading" a private religious group. Even though most agreed that Koresh was directly responsible for the deaths, they felt the government had mishandled the situation.

In the days following the Waco tragedy, the following question was asked: Why did the government try a drastic tactic like an armed assault when they believed Koresh was mentally unstable? It seemed like a foolish idea. This incident reflected poorly on Clinton's instincts as a leader.

Clinton did receive credit for appointing a diverse Cabinet. He claimed its diversity "looks like America."[7] He selected: a woman, Janet Reno, to be attorney general; a Hispanic-American, Henry Cisneros, as head of Housing and Urban Development; an African American, Mike Espy, as secretary of agriculture; and an African-American woman, Joycelyn Elders, as surgeon general. He also brought some boyhood friends with him to serve on his staff. One was Vince Foster, his personal lawyer, who had worked with Hillary at the Rose Law Firm.

Yet as 1993 progressed, Clinton appeared to be weak and wishy-washy. Analysts began calling Clinton a "waffler," or someone who fails to make strong decisions. It seemed to be taking forever to develop his plan for health care reform. Republicans condemned Clinton for raising taxes. Most of these were directed at the richest Americans, traditionally among the Republican party's most powerful supporters.

Then in July, tragedy hit the administration at close range. Vince Foster, Clinton's lawyer, had been working an unhealthy amount of long hours and was being treated by a doctor for depression. On July 17, the *Wall Street Journal* ran an editorial blasting Foster's legal abilities. Three days later, Foster drove to a Washington park and shot himself to death. The president was very upset, but he buried himself in his work.

One issue he was working on would split his own party. It would also gain him support from Republicans. The idea was called NAFTA. The letters stood for North American Free Trade Agreement.

When nations trade with each other, they often charge a tax, called a tariff, on goods imported from other countries. The addition of this tariff makes foreign products more expensive than similar domestic products.

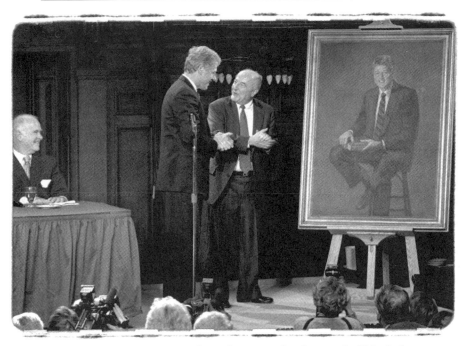

President Clinton receives the Yale Law School Award of Merit from the dean of Yale Law School, Guido Calabresi, on the occasion of the President's 20th law school reunion in 1993.

The purpose is to motivate people to buy the less expensive American-made products, thereby saving the American businesses and their workers' jobs.

NAFTA was to remove all tariffs existing between any two of North America's three nations: Canada, the United States, and Mexico. American labor unions, which traditionally vote Democratic, were against NAFTA. They felt that without the tariffs' protection, American businesses might move to Mexico where they could pay workers less money and therefore make greater profits. They also believed Americans would buy cheaper foreign products if they were available.

On the other hand, a lot of Republicans supported

NAFTA. They argued that quality products do not need special protection. In addition, they said that NAFTA would open up a whole new range of foreign products for American consumers to buy.

As NAFTA was being debated in Congress, Clinton was by chance given a different role on the world stage. The roots to this event go back to 1948. That year, Israel was declared a nation by the United Nations. Finally, Jews had a homeland where they could live under their own rule. A problem was what to do with the Arabs, known as Palestinians, who were already living there. Most were Muslim and some were Christian, but most did not want to live in Israel now that it was a Jewish state.

Once Israel became a nation, many Palestinians lived in the country of Jordan on the West Bank of the Jordan River (known simply as the "West Bank") under Israeli rule. The leader of the Palestinians, Yasir Arafat, led terrorist attacks against innocent Israelis for decades. For that reason, among others, Israel's leaders refused to have anything to do with Arafat and the Palestinians.

By the 1990s, a large number of Israelis believed the only way to have peace was to sit down with their enemies. They said there would never be peace unless someone had the courage to negotiate with Arafat.

Israel's prime minister, Yitzhak Rabin, was that person. With the help of diplomats from Norway, Rabin and Arafat came to an agreement in September 1993. Israel would return land in the West Bank so the Palestinians could live there under their own rule. In exchange, Arafat and the Palestinians would stop all their terrorist attacks against Israelis and accept Israel's right to exist in peace.

Because the United States has always played a role in

Middle Eastern affairs, Rabin and Arafat decided to sign their agreement in an official ceremony at the White House. The date was September 13, 1993. Former presidents Jimmy Carter and George Bush were in attendance. There were also dignitaries present from countries around the world. It was a perfect chance for President Clinton to step into the role of world leader.

NBC news correspondent Tom Brokaw said of the happy ceremony, "It has all the elements . . . of a bar mitzvah and an Arab wedding, all presided over by a Baptist from Arkansas."[8] Clinton vowed to work with Israel and other Arab countries such as Jordan and Syria. By many

Clinton plays host to Israeli prime minister Yitzhak Rabin (left) and Palestinian leader Yasir Arafat (right). The two Middle Eastern dignitaries signed an historic peace agreement at the White House on September 13, 1993.

accounts, it was the first time Clinton appeared to the world to be truly presidential.

Two weeks later, on September 27, the Clinton health care plan was finally introduced. It was complicated, but basically it meant that if Congress approved the plan, every American would be covered by health insurance.

Such broad insurance would be expensive. Who would pay for it? Clinton's plan provided that each working person's employer would pay for most of it, and each state would pay for the insurance of residents of the state who were unemployed.

At first, Americans were strongly in favor of the plan. Then critics began asking tough questions. Most big companies could afford to pay for insurance for their employees, but money was a tougher problem for small businesses. Some small business owners claimed they would have to lay off some workers in order to be able to pay for the insurance for others.

At the same time, private insurance companies were concerned about losing business. They spent a lot of money on advertisements making the false claim that under Clinton's plan people might lose the right to choose their own doctors. Critics also complained that this health care plan represented nothing more than another typical Democratic big-spending, big-government idea. Many Americans listened to these criticisms and began doubting that Clinton's health care plan would work.

One of the Clinton plan's most vocal critics was an ultraconservative radio broadcaster named Rush Limbaugh. On Limbaugh's national daily radio program, listeners called in to voice their opinions. By 1993, Limbaugh had the highest-rated national program on radio, and he had become a thorn in the sides of the president and the first lady. Limbaugh urged his radio listeners to show up and personally protest the Clintons when they appeared in public to promote the health care plan. Limbaugh's techniques were very effective, and the protesters became an embarrassment for the first couple. The Clintons had much convincing to do.

Outside the United States, Clinton had other problems to attend to. Even though Iraq had lost the Gulf War, its leader, Saddam Hussein, was still in power. Part of the agreement that ended the war stated that Iraq would agree to let United Nations inspectors visit its military facilities. The inspectors were to see whether Iraq was complying with its promise to stop manufacturing danger- ous weapons. Despite this promise, Saddam was not always willing to let U.N. representatives do their jobs. Clinton was constantly posted on Saddam's moves. If Saddam acted recklessly, it could mean another war against Iraq.

Troubles were not limited to the Persian Gulf. Another hot spot was the Balkans region of Eastern Europe. The history of this conflict went back many decades. Following World War I (1914–1918), several small nations that were heavily involved in the war had joined together to form the nation of Yugoslavia.

Yugoslavia became a Communist nation. After the Soviet empire crumbled in 1989, Yugoslavia broke up into smaller countries. These were similar to the countries that had existed before World War I. All the hard feelings that were under control while Yugoslavia was united as one nation rose to the surface. Now there was war between these peoples all over again.

One of these nations is Serbia. Serbia is mainly Christian. Another is Bosnia, which is mostly Muslim. The two nations began fighting again in 1992. In this case, Serbia was the aggressor country. The Serbs were accused of massacring innocent Bosnian civilians simply because they were Muslims and not Serbs.

What should Clinton do? Some advisers agreed that although the situation in Bosnia was horrible, American servicemen should not fight in a war that had no bearing on the security of the United States. There was always the ghost of Vietnam. If Clinton sent Americans to fight in Bosnia, would he be getting his country involved in a long, drawn-out conflict like the one he had so daringly protested in the 1960s?

Others disagreed: Their position was that as decent human beings, Americans should not stand by and do nothing when genocide, or the mass destruction of an ethnic group, is taking place. These people compared the Balkan situation to the Holocaust in World War II. Still others felt the United States had a legitimate interest in the war: If nothing were done to stop the fighting, it might spread to other countries in Eastern Europe—countries in which the United States had vital interests.

Finally, after months of discussions with advisers and world leaders, in late May the president decided to send three hundred American troops to a former part of Yugoslavia called Macedonia.[9] They would work with the United Nations Protection Forces and help troops from other nations try to keep the conflict from spreading.

Clinton inherited another world conflict from President Bush. Bush had sent United States troops to Somalia, a nation in eastern Africa involved in a brutal civil war. The United States had not been directly affected in any way by this conflict. However, scores of Somalian citizens were starving as a result of the civil war. As was the case with Bosnia, some Americans felt their country could not justifiably sit back and watch masses of innocent people suffer.

Originally, American troops had been sent to Somalia in December 1992 to help needy people receive food and supplies. However, by the fall of 1993, it was clear that the United States troops had themselves become involved in the fighting. The Americans were trying to capture a Somalian warlord named Mohammed Farah Aideed.

They were not succeeding. While watching the evening news on the night of October 3, Americans were sickened. They saw the naked body of a dead American serviceman dragged through the streets by Somalian gangs. Americans demanded that their troops be withdrawn before more horrors happened to their men.

At the same time, there were troubles closer to home. Haiti, a nation on the island of Hispaniola in the Caribbean Sea, had never been blessed with a stable government. For decades its people were ruled by a dictatorship. In 1990, Haiti held its first democratic election, and a man named Jean-Bertrand Aristide was elected president. Just nine months later, he was overthrown by Haiti's military strongmen who took over the nation's leadership.

Almost immediately, boatloads of Haitians who did not want to live under a military dictator began to flee their country. Most of these refugees landed in Florida. Since they had not entered the United States legally, Florida and United States authorities did not know what to do with them. It appeared that the Haitian situation might repeat the disaster President Carter had experienced with Cuban refugees fifteen year earlier.

To stop the flow of refugees, the United States helped Aristide and the military leaders come to an agreement in June. Aristide was to return to power on October 30, 1993. Hopefully, the flood of Haitian refugees to the United States would end. In return, the United Nations would supply Haiti with American military personnel who would help Haiti's military build bridges, schools, and roads.

In early October, it became clear that Haiti's military leaders were not going to live up to their end of the agreement. The United States sent military trainers on a boat called the *Harlan County*. It arrived in Haiti on October 11. An armed mob of dozens of demonstrators met the boat. The American trainers had come in peace and were not well armed. Haiti's police and military could not guarantee the Americans' safety. The next day the *Harlan County* left Haiti to head home. It looked to the world as if a small gang of Haitian rioters had managed to scare away the mighty United States military forces. The United States then began to negotiate all over again with the Haitian military.

While Clinton was occupied with serious situations in the world's trouble spots, his pen was busy at home. One of the most controversial new laws he signed was the Brady Law. It was named for James Brady, President Ronald Reagan's press secretary. Brady was seriously injured and paralyzed by a gunshot in an assassination attempt on Reagan's life in 1981. Afterward, Brady and his wife, Sarah, worked for years to pass a strict gun-control law. The Brady Law requires a five-day waiting period for people purchasing handguns so that background checks can be made on the gun purchasers. If it is learned that a gun buyer is potentially dangerous, he or she is not allowed to buy the gun.

The Family and Medical Leave Act was another law passed during Clinton's first year. Until the law was passed, a person who took days off from work to care for a sick child or an elderly parent could be fired from his or her job. The new law made firing a person under such circumstances illegal.

There was also the National Voter Registration Act. It was known by a slang name, the "Motor Voter Act." The law enabled people to register to vote when they went to a local motor vehicle agency to get a driver's license. They could also register to vote through the mail and at some public assistance offices.

Clinton boosters were thrilled at all the legislation his administration passed. However, critics of the president were growing in number. A conservative newspaper, *The Washington Times*, reported that Hillary Rodham Clinton had removed files from Vince Foster's office after his death. The reason, the report claimed, was that some information in those files could be damaging to the Clintons. Clinton's enemies were even spreading rumors that Vince Foster did not kill himself but instead had been murdered under orders by the president and first lady. Most Americans thought such accusations were nonsense.

In addition, the Whitewater scandal was rearing its head. In 1993 who could have foreseen that this years-old real estate matter would lead to only the second presidential impeachment in history?

8

THE FALL AND RISE OF BILL CLINTON

In February 1994, Paula Jones came forward with her claim that Clinton had sexually harassed her in a Little Rock hotel in 1991. Democrats immediately attacked her and her supporters, accusing them of making up a false charge to embarrass the president.

There was reason to believe this might be true. Some ultraconservative people and organizations were supporting Jones morally and financially. They included radio personality Rush Limbaugh and the radical anti-abortion group Operation Rescue. Others helping Jones were right-wing television evangelists Jerry Falwell and Pat Robertson. In the past, these people had accused the National Organization for Women (NOW) and feminist supporters of being responsible for many of America's social ills. Now, suddenly, these same critics of feminism were defending a woman on a feminist issue.

At the same time, Whitewater refused to go away. Republicans still demanded answers to questions about the Clintons' financial dealings years ago. They also wanted to know whether the Clintons were trying to hinder the current investigation into these dealings. If so, it would be considered a case of obstruction of justice.

Republicans in Congress demanded that something be done to get to the bottom of the situation. They urged Attorney General Janet Reno to name an independent

Paula Jones, who accused Clinton of sexual harassment, was backed by right-wing conservatives who did not share the same political views as the president.

prosecutor to look into the Whitewater matter. For this job, Reno selected a moderate Republican lawyer named Robert B. Fiske, Jr.

While the investigation into Whitewater was taking place, the nation's business went on as usual. Both Clintons spent much of 1994 trying to stir up support for their health care plan, which came under increasing criticism. Leon Panetta, who held two different roles in the Clinton administration, explained:

> First, the plan was very complex to understand. Second, there was a failure to get a consensus [an agreement] from Capitol Hill [Congress]. We should have built it up in increments instead of presenting it all at once. There were also opponents who attacked it as a kind of socialism. It wasn't any kind of socialism. But people were naturally afraid of what they did not understand. The opponents created fear of what was involved.[1]

In the summer of 1994, Congress killed the plan. After all their time and energy, the Clintons had nothing to show for their work.

Clinton had better success with other legislation. Polls showed Americans were deeply concerned about the spread of crime. Clinton proposed a bill that called for tougher sentences for convicted criminals, more police, and more prisons. As was the case with NAFTA, dozens of Democrats in Congress disagreed with Clinton. Many were against the death penalty, and others felt the proposed tougher sentences might be too severe. They voted against his crime bill. At first, not enough Republicans made up the difference, and the bill was defeated.

Clinton did not give up, however. He proposed a new crime bill, stronger than the first one. It called for the death penalty for crimes such as car-jacking and drive-by shooting. It also mandated a life sentence for any person convicted in his or her lifetime of three violent crimes. To appeal to Democrats, the bill included a ban on nineteen types of assault weapons. There had been an outbreak of mass murders in recent years committed by persons using assault weapons such as AK-47s.

As with the Brady Law, gun owners and their supporters were disgusted by the idea of an assault weapons ban. The biggest lobbying group supporting gun owners' rights is the National Rifle Association (NRA). It opposes any regulation of gun ownership. The NRA is known for giving large amounts of financial aid to its supporters in Congress. Most are Republicans. Still, enough Republicans crossed over and voted with the Democrats to pass the crime bill on August 21, 1994.

Clinton had one more success with Congress. Once again, it meant losing support from members of his own party. The bill was called the General Agreement on Tariffs and Trade (GATT). Instead of being limited to North America like NAFTA, GATT was an agreement made by nations around the globe. The result of GATT is free trade throughout much of the world.

By the fall of 1994, the American public generally viewed Clinton as weak in the area of foreign affairs. Perhaps it was by comparison with his predecessor, George Bush, who had led the United States to a dramatic victory in war. Actually, Clinton had successes in foreign policy. One involved Haiti. With help from former president Jimmy Carter and retired general Colin Powell, the military regime that had seized power in Haiti agreed to leave office in September. Aristide was reinstalled as president, and Haitian refugees were returned from the United States to their homeland. The United States sent twenty thousand troops to Haiti to help maintain peace.[2]

On the other side of the world, the Communist nation of North Korea was accused of refining plutonium, a radioactive element, to make nuclear weapons. An international agreement, called the Nuclear Nonproliferation Treaty (NPT), banned the manufacture of such weapons. North Korea appeared to be in direct violation of the NPT. The United States had been at war with North Korea before in the early fifties. Suddenly there was talk of a second Korean War.

Clinton and his advisers discussed sanctions, or penalties, against North Korea. Again Clinton prevailed, with the help of former President Carter. North Korea agreed to stop further nuclear activity. The Communist country also allowed official inspectors into its military facilities to check and make sure it was keeping its part of the deal. The United States dropped all talk of sanctions, and war with North Korea was avoided.

In spite of these successes, President Clinton's approval rating was dropping. Foreign affairs don't usually affect people's personal lives in as direct a way as the economy. Americans were more concerned with their pocketbooks at home than with their successes overseas. Citizens who had voted for Clinton started to think he had betrayed them. Clinton had campaigned for president as a "new Democrat," promising that the nation would no longer need to rely on big, expensive government programs. Yet his failed health care plan seemed to be just that.

In addition, Clinton could not escape the fallout from

Whitewater. At first, the matter seemed to have subsided. Special Prosecutor Robert Fiske concluded that Vince Foster was not murdered as Clinton critics claimed. Fiske also reported that his investigation had discovered no criminal behavior on the part of the Clintons concerning the Whitewater matter.

Still, Republicans were not satisfied with this conclusion. They wanted someone else to investigate the matter further. A panel of three judges appointed an attorney named Kenneth Starr to be an independent counsel. Starr immediately reopened the Vince Foster case to see if Foster had been murdered.

Starr is a stronger conservative than Fiske. There was talk that he could not be objective or impartial. As a private attorney, Starr had written a legal brief on behalf of a conservative group supporting Paula Jones. In addition, he worked as a lawyer for the Brown and Williamson tobacco company. At the time, Clinton was attacking tobacco companies for directing their advertisements at young people.

The question was asked: Did Republicans really want the truth about Whitewater, or did they simply want to damage and embarrass Clinton any way they could? Some critics wondered if the Republicans weren't really after revenge for the Watergate scandal, during which many Democrats enthusiastically attacked Republican president Richard Nixon, eventually causing him to resign.

Richard Nixon was probably the most hated president of the last few generations. However, some say attacks on Clinton have been more brutal than those on Nixon. It is a small but vocal minority that holds such intense feelings toward Clinton. But why?

Attorney Kenneth Starr was the second independent counsel appointed to investigate allegations of misconduct by the Clintons in the Whitewater matter. Many Democrats questioned his impartiality.

Former Clinton chief of staff Leon Panetta explains,

> It's a cloud that seems to hang over him [Clinton] and goes back to his political career in Arkansas. There were rumors then that he burned a [American] flag while in Britain protesting the war [in Vietnam]. It has continued since then. These are started by people who have resented his success and the work he has done on [controversial] issues.[3]

Panetta believes that being the first postwar baby boomer president added to Clinton's negative image. "I think he is kind of representative of that generation, and some resent it. People think they [baby boomers] had everything easy and didn't have to work for it."[4]

Midterm congressional elections were to take place in November 1994. Mainstream Republicans used Clinton's failed health care plan to paint him as just another traditional Democrat who supported big government. The National Rifle Association worked hard to defeat legislators who supported Clinton's gun-control laws. Those plans worked. On Election Day, the Republicans swept to majorities in both the Senate and the House of Representatives, for the first time since the 1950s. Georgia representative Newt Gingrich was chosen by his party to be Speaker of the House, or head of the majority party in Congress, a powerful position.

The Republican sweep in Congress was embarrassing for Clinton. Now, instead of the president proposing laws and presenting them to Congress for approval, Congress was proposing laws and passing them on to the president. The Congress, not the president, appeared to be in charge of the nation's political agenda. At a press conference held on April 18, 1995, a reporter asked Clinton to comment on that situation. Weakly, the president responded that he was still "relevant."[5]

On the very next day, an unforeseen tragedy of huge proportions showed that the president was indeed still relevant. On the morning of April 19, a terrorist bomb destroyed a building in downtown Oklahoma City. The building was home to government office workers and a day care center filled with children who had just sat down to eat breakfast. Pictures on television and in newspapers showed survivors outside the building covered with blood. One widely circulated photograph was of a firefighter holding a dying baby in his arms. A total of one hundred sixty-nine people died in the bombing, including nineteen children.[6]

Americans were grief-stricken by the cowardly act. That night, President Clinton spoke to the horrified nation. With carefully chosen words, he addressed the people's fears and sorrows. He promised "swift and certain and severe" punishment for the bombers. Clinton tried to soothe the traumatized nation. Many observers believe it was the first time in his presidency that Clinton showed true leadership.

At first, it was suspected that anti-American Islamic terrorists from the Middle East were responsible. Then evidence began shifting toward two American men with connections to right-wing antigovernment groups: Timothy McVeigh and Terry Nichols were later convicted. Later, it was revealed they had planned this crime to take place on April 19, the second anniversary of the fire/suicide at the Branch-Davidian compound outside Waco, Texas.

In the following months, Clinton continued to push his economic plan. There were no more "big government ideas" such as the health care reform plan. Clinton made it clear that both he and Congress supported the same goals: a balanced federal budget and smaller government. However, they had different ways of trying to achieve those goals. The Republican-controlled Congress wanted to balance the budget in seven years. Clinton wanted to take nine years. The Republicans wanted to cut even more government programs than Clinton.

In a strange way, the election of the Republican

Congress in 1994 turned out to be a blessing in disguise for Clinton. He used his presidential power to veto one Republican bill after another. He looked strong, and his "waffler" image began to fade away.

At first, the Republicans' promises of reducing big government spending and cutting government programs sounded wonderful. Then Americans stopped to think. Maybe they did not want government completely out of their lives. Maybe they did not want to lose big government programs such as Social Security and Medicare. Social Security, begun by Franklin Roosevelt, is a retirement savings plan. Medicare, started by Lyndon Johnson, allows elderly persons to have free medical care. Because of both programs, America's elderly are at their healthiest and wealthiest levels ever.

The Republican Congress learned something else. Now that they had power, its members faced the same intense personal scrutiny that the president had. Speaker of the House Newt Gingrich's personal life was being examined just as closely as Clinton's had been, and not all the details were flattering. A story about an ugly incident in Gingrich's past was soon publicized.

Gingrich's first wife, Jackie, had undergone breast cancer surgery some years earlier. One story said that while she was groggy from the effects of the anesthesia, Gingrich forced her to sign divorce papers. Gingrich and his supporters responded that the story had been exaggerated by liberals in the media.

Because Clinton's ideas on making government smaller and more efficient were similar to those of Republicans, he began to lose the confidence of traditional Democrats. At the same time, African Americans and other minorities felt

Clinton was deserting them. Racial minorities traditionally view government programs as essential in helping to keep poor people living above the poverty level.

Clinton wanted to make it clear that he was not a Republican in disguise. He especially did not want to be challenged for the Democratic party nomination in 1996. True, Clinton was the sitting president, but that advantage did not automatically guarantee him the nomination from his party.

That summer, the president took to the world stage again. Bosnia was being attacked by Serbia. The North Atlantic Treaty Organization (NATO) is a military alliance of the United States and several European nations. On August 30, Clinton rallied the NATO nations to start a campaign of air strikes against Serbian military posts.

Just eight days later, the outline of a peace agreement between the warring nations was announced. On October 5, a cease-fire was ordered in Bosnia. The next month, representatives of the warring nations met at Wright-Patterson Air Force Base in Dayton, Ohio, to iron out a final peace agreement. One was reached on November 21.

It was also agreed that the United States and other nations would send troops to the area to help keep peace. Americans were concerned about sending their soldiers to an unstable part of the world. Again, some voiced concern about whether the United States should get involved in what might become a European version of the Vietnam War. Clinton stemmed those fears by promising that troops would be withdrawn by the end of 1996.

Although the calendar year runs from January through December, businesses and other organizations run on what is called a fiscal year, a twelve-month period in which a group measures its finances. The United States government's fiscal year begins on the first day in October and ends on the last day of September. The president and Congress have to approve a budget for the government to operate from one fiscal year to the next.

In the fall of 1995, the president and Congress could not come to an agreement on the federal budget for October 1995 through September 1996. If they could not agree by October 1, the government would not technically be granted money to operate.

October 1 came and went. There was no agreement. An extension on the deadline was passed to keep the government operating. Talks between Congress and the president went on. Finally, at midnight on November 13, all nonvital operations of the federal government were closed. A total of eight hundred thousand government employees were told to go home.[7] The national parks were closed, so vacationers could not visit them. The Social Security office was closed, so citizens' checks could not be processed. Americans began to realize just how much they needed the federal government.

A day later, the American public learned one reason behind the shutdown. A week earlier Clinton, former presidents Jimmy Carter and George Bush, Speaker Newt Gingrich, and Senate Majority Leader Robert Dole had flown to Israel to attend the funeral of Israeli prime minister Yitzhak Rabin.

During the long flight, Clinton spent some of his time talking with Bush and Carter. He never went to the rear of the plane to visit with Gingrich and Dole. This lack of social protocol did not bother Dole, but Gingrich was outraged. He considered Clinton's snub an insult.[8]

Speaker of the House Newt Gingrich, a powerful Republican, made it difficult for Clinton to keep the government operating.

In response to this social snub, Gingrich did everything he could to persuade Congress to make it difficult for Clinton to keep the government operating. Finally, Clinton had no choice but to shut the government down.

Gingrich soon became a target of criticism. Some of it was mean-spirited. On its cover, the *New York Daily News* ran a cartoon of Gingrich wearing a diaper and holding a baby bottle in his hand. Tears were falling down his face. The headline read, "CRY BABY." Underneath, the caption read, "NEWT'S TANTRUM: He closed down the government because Clinton made him sit at back of plane."[9]

An extension to keep the government running was passed on November 20. Government employees returned to work. However, the extension expired on December 16, and the federal government was shut down once more. Citizens were frustrated. Opinion polls showed that twice as many people blamed Gingrich and Congress as blamed Clinton.[10] The president looked good.

As confident as Gingrich had been in January 1995, he was just that humble by December. The year ended with President Bill Clinton standing tall in the White House.

9

FEELING GOOD AT ELECTION TIME

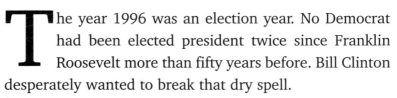

T he year 1996 was an election year. No Democrat had been elected president twice since Franklin Roosevelt more than fifty years before. Bill Clinton desperately wanted to break that dry spell.

The conditions of 1996 made it easier for Clinton than for previous Democrats in office. The United States was at peace, and the nation was enjoying real prosperity.

Clinton had another benefit. No Democrat had come forward to challenge him for the nomination. Vice-President Gore campaigned hard for Clinton and was respected by his fellow Democrats. With his party united behind Clinton, the president looked in control.

Still, Clinton's road to a second term was not without pitfalls. The Whitewater scandal was still brewing, and a Senate committee was conducting hearings on the matter. Interestingly, the Whitewater charges against the Clintons did not seem to bother the majority of Americans. Some found the case, which was mainly about investments and financial loans, too confusing to understand fully. Others felt an event that had happened years before Clinton took office was not that relevant, even if the Clintons had tried to cover up evidence while in office. Most of these citizens were more concerned with their own financial security.

In June, the Senate Whitewater Committee finished its hearings. The committee chairman, Republican senator Al D'Amato, issued a report highly critical of the Clintons' actions and supposed dishonesty. However, it did not accuse either Clinton of any criminal act.

Yet Whitewater was not over. Independent Counsel Kenneth Starr was still running his own investigation. In a separate trial on a different matter, Clinton's Whitewater financial partners, James and Susan McDougal, were convicted of fraud. The Arkansas governor, Jim Guy Tucker, was convicted, too. The Clintons were not directly involved in this unrelated case, but some people felt they were guilty by association.

In mid-August 1996, the Republicans held their national convention in San Diego. Senate Majority Leader Bob Dole was officially nominated by the Republican party for president. Dole chose New York congressperson Jack Kemp as his running mate.

On August 22, Clinton signed another law that departed from traditional Democratic views: a welfare reform law. To many working-class Americans, it was welcome. The law put a time limit on government financial assistance to unemployed welfare recipients. By signing this law, Clinton took an issue away from the Republicans, who were traditionally critical of welfare, and made it his own.

Four days after Clinton signed the welfare reform law, the Democrats met in Chicago for their convention. Clinton and Gore were easily renominated by their party with virtually no opposition.

Polls showed Clinton with a heavy lead over Dole. In campaign commercials, the Democrats went beyond praising Clinton. They linked Dole to unpopular House Speaker Newt Gingrich. Leon Panetta offered another reason why Clinton looked strong. He said, "The battle over the budget in 1995 that led to the Republicans shutting down the government showed the American people the contrast between the two parties. Clinton wouldn't back down and compromise. He showed the Republicans that he wasn't wishy-washy and would stand for something."[1] To many, the government shutdown also made the Republicans appear mean-spirited and vengeful.

Dole promised the voters a 15 percent cut in their income taxes. Americans had doubts about whether that was a good idea. They feared it would make the national deficit, which is money the government owes, bigger and reverse the progress being made in reducing the deficit for the first time in decades.

With the economy responding to Clinton's budget cuts and the nation's low unemployment rate, the Democrats felt confident. They had reason to. On November 5, Clinton and Gore were reelected. Clinton received 379 electoral votes while Dole earned 159.[2] In the popular vote, Clinton picked up 49.3 percent of the total. Dole had 40.7 percent. Third-party candidate Ross Perot was a minor factor this time. He received only 8.4 percent.[3]

No sooner was the election over when another scandal hit the Clinton administration. Now the Democrats were accused of raising illegal campaign funds. By the end of November, the Democrats had returned over a million dollars in campaign contributions.

Then Clinton announced that he could not keep his promise about bringing American troops home from Bosnia by the end of 1996. He claimed that the Americans, as part of the NATO Stabilization Force, were still needed in Europe and would stay until June 1998. One thing was certain: this was not another Vietnam. Americans were involved in little fighting.

Several of Clinton's Cabinet members resigned after the first term was finished. Most were simply tired of their jobs and politics in general. Clinton continued to assemble a Cabinet that "looked like America." He chose the first woman ever to be secretary of state, Madeleine Albright. He also picked a Republican to be secretary of defense, Senator William Cohen of Maine.

Scandals about financial wrongdoings hit the Republicans, too, the next month. House Speaker Newt Gingrich was found guilty of misusing campaign donations. He was fined $300,000 and reprimanded.

The Democrats had nothing to gloat about since they continued to be accused of accepting illegal campaign donations. In question was money taken from foreign citizens and businesses, including businessmen from China and Indonesia. The concern was that by giving money to help elect the president, these nations could unfairly influence American foreign policy.

However, campaign financing regulations are very complex. What is technically a violation can be easily disputed. In April 1997, Attorney General Janet Reno refused to appoint an independent counsel to investigate

Madeleine Albright was chosen by Clinton at the start of his second term to be secretary of state. She was the first woman ever to hold this Cabinet post.

the matter. She said there was not enough evidence that serious illegal acts had been committed.

In 1997, Clinton and the Republican-led Congress came to an agreement to balance the federal budget by 2002. It would be the first balanced budget in over thirty years. Clinton pushed through Congress a bill creating more government scholarships to young people attending college. He urged eight major gun manufacturers to put child-safety devices on all handguns sold, and they agreed. Clinton also continued to attack the tobacco industry. He threatened to fine cigarette makers who aimed the marketing of their products toward young people.

These accomplishments made it more difficult for Clinton's enemies to attack his legislation. Therefore, they continued to attack his character. At times it seemed that Clinton's opponents found scandal when there was none. Arlington National Cemetery in Virginia is a burial site for military veterans. However, a president can give special permission to bury a nonveteran there if the person has done a heroic deed.

In November, Rush Limbaugh and other conservatives claimed that Clinton had allowed certain nonveterans to be buried at Arlington because they had contributed money to the Democrats. The mainstream media picked up on the story. It looked as if another scandal was about to hit the Clinton White House. After looking into the matter, the newspaper *USA Today* stated, "There was just one problem with the latest Democratic campaign finance scandal. None of it could be proved."[4]

Of the sixty-nine nonveterans Clinton tried to have buried in Arlington, it was discovered that only one had been a major contributor to the Democratic party.[5] Perhaps that is why, by the late 1990s, the American public tired of all the talk about scandals. Yet in January 1998 one more scandal arose. This was the one that would lead all the way to impeachment and threaten to remove Bill Clinton from office.

10

IMPEACHMENT

The story began with Linda Tripp, a White House employee who was first hired as a staff worker when George Bush was president. She stayed on after Clinton was elected. Tripp became friendly with a woman hired as a White House intern, Monica Lewinsky. As friends often do, Lewinsky and Tripp confided in each other. At times, in their conversations, Lewinsky revealed details about having a romantic affair with the president.

What Lewinsky did not know was that when the two women met or talked on the phone, Tripp was secretly tape-recording their conversations. Whitewater independent prosecutor Kenneth Starr had given her permission to do so. Some say he had even directed her to do so. Tripp turned over these explosive tapes to Starr, and news of the alleged affair between the president and the intern was reported first on the Internet, then in *The Washington Post* on January 21, 1998.

While investigating the Paula Jones case earlier, Starr had asked Lewinsky whether she had had a sexual affair with the president. Lewinsky swore under oath that she had never had an affair with Clinton. That statement and her recorded conversations with Tripp contradicted each other. If Lewinsky had lied under oath, she had committed perjury, a crime for which she could go to jail.

Some observers questioned why independent counsel Starr was investigating the Paula Jones case in the first place. He had been hired to look into Whitewater. Neither the Paula Jones case nor the Lewinsky matter was related at all to Whitewater. Starr answered his critics by claiming that he was trying to find a pattern of deceit in the president's conduct.

In answer to the public's growing curiosity, Clinton stated he never had an improper relationship with Lewinsky. He responded to a television reporter on January 26 by stating in very strong words that he had never had an affair with "that woman." The filmed clip was shown repeatedly on national television that night and over the next several days.

The media tried to outdo one another in getting every fact and nuance about this sexual scandal involving the married president and the woman less than half his age. There was talk that Clinton had not only carried on a romantic relationship with Lewinsky, but during an investigation had asked her to lie about it if she were questioned by jurors investigating the matter. If so, Clinton would be guilty of obstructing justice. Some felt Clinton had no way out of this dilemma. One journalist, Sam

Donaldson, of ABC News, predicted Clinton would resign within a week.

On January 27, Clinton delivered his State of the Union address for 1998. He did not mention the scandal, and the speech was well-received. It was clear that despite his public embarrassment, Clinton was not planning to leave the White House any time soon.

Meanwhile, many people were having more doubts than ever about independent counsel Kenneth Starr's motives and his tactics. People were questioning whether it was legal for Tripp to have secretly taped Lewinsky. If not illegal, her actions certainly seemed to be unethical. It appeared that Lewinsky had been set up, or entrapped. Again, Americans wondered, was Starr looking for justice, or was he just determined to hurt Clinton?

The public had trouble believing Starr. In February, a poll showed that 53 percent of the public agreed with the statement that Starr is "out to get Clinton whatever it takes, fair or unfair."[1] A different poll showed that 59 percent of the public believed that Starr's investigation should be stopped.[2]

By the beginning of 1998, White House intern Monica Lewinsky was rumored to have had an affair with Clinton.

Meanwhile, Clinton and his lawyers were getting ready to face Paula Jones in court. Her sexual harassment case was finally set for trial in May. On April 1, Clinton heard welcoming news. A judge threw out, or dismissed, the Jones case. Judge Susan Webber Wright declared flatly in a federal district court in Little Rock, Arkansas, "There are no genuine issues for trial in this case."[3] When Clinton heard the good news, he asked if it was an April Fool's Day joke. It was no joke.

The next day, a *New York Times* writer stated, "It is now politically inconceivable that Congress will consider impeachment—for President Clinton's alleged lies and obstruction in a case that no longer exists."[4]

In spite of all the questionable conduct Clinton had been accused of over the years—draft dodging, lying, raising campaign money dishonestly, and being unfaithful to his wife—he remained a popular president. A poll conducted in mid-April showed his approval rating at an amazing 67 percent.[5]

The rating did not mean Americans approved of everything about the president. One poll released at about the same time showed that 34 percent of the public assessed his character as "average," and 35 percent described his character as low or very low.[6] Pollster Fred Yang said, "As long as people are feeling good, they are willing to say they approve the job he's doing despite the concerns about his character."[7]

Americans were feeling very good in the spring of 1998. The economy was still strong, and the crime rate was dropping for the fifth year in a row. Clinton's welfare reform law inspired the formation of a group called the Welfare to Work Partnership. It helped private companies hire former welfare recipients. A survey taken in May 1998 showed that one hundred thirty-five thousand former welfare recipients had been hired by private businesses over the past year.[8]

Then again, some of Clinton's supporters were just tired of Kenneth Starr and his investigation. By 1998, it had dragged on for over four years. It had cost the nation over $40 million, and there was still no end in sight.

That spring, an article appeared in *Esquire* magazine, written by a conservative columnist named David Brock. It seemed to prove Clinton supporters' suspicions—that ultraconservatives were out to get the president any way they could. Democrats gleefully seized upon the article as evidence that they had been right all along.

The article was written in the form of an open letter to Clinton. Basically, it was a long apology by Brock to Clinton for his part in damaging the president. Brock blamed himself for having been the first person to discuss publicly the idea that Clinton had had an improper affair with a woman whose first name was Paula.

In the *Esquire* article, Brock wrote to Clinton, "Surveying the wreckage that my report has wrought four years later, I've asked myself over and over: What the hell was I doing investigating your private life in the first place?"[9] Later in the article, Brock answered his own question: "I never felt the visceral hatred toward you that many of your detractors harbor, but I did regard you, the first Democratic president in my adult life, as a . . . threat."[10]

In May, Clinton once more starred on the world stage. With the president's approval, an American envoy helped arrange a peace agreement between the Republic of Ireland and Northern Ireland which had been at war for decades. Even to his enemies, Clinton seemed to be a gifted diplomat.

There was further evidence that Clinton's domestic policies were working, too. A government study reported that due to the passage of the Brady gun-control law, roughly sixty-nine thousand felons, drug addicts, and fugitives were stopped from buying handguns in 1997. The United States Justice Department also reported that since the Brady law had gone into effect in 1994, a total of nearly two hundred forty-two thousand gun purchases were prevented because of the law's mandatory background checks.[11]

Yet throughout the rest of 1998, news about issues took a backseat to the Lewinsky scandal. Developments came fast and furious. Nearly all had a negative impact of some kind on the president.

On July 28, Kenneth Starr offered Monica Lewinsky full immunity, or freedom from punishment for any crimes she had previously committed. In exchange for immunity, she agreed to tell the independent counsel the entire truth about her relationship with the president.

Just three days later Paula Jones and her lawyers made it clear they were not going away. They asked an appeals court to reinstate her case against Clinton. For Clinton, it was as if Judge Wright's decision to drop the case had never happened. He was going to have to deal with Paula Jones all over again.

Within a week, on August 6, Lewinsky testified to a grand jury that she had had a sexual relationship with Clinton. However, she added that the president never told her to lie about it. Physical evidence made it clear that Clinton and Lewinsky did indeed have an affair. Finally,

Clinton had no choice but to tell the truth, which he did to a grand jury on August 17. That night, he spoke again to the American people on television.

Referring to the grand jury's questions, Clinton said,

> This afternoon, in this room, from this chair I answered questions no American citizen would ever want to answer. But I must take responsibility for all my actions, public and private. I did have a relationship with Monica Lewinsky that was not appropriate. Indeed, it was wrong. It constituted a lapse of judgment and personal failure on my part for which I am solely and completely responsible.[12]

He added "this matter is between me, the two people I love most—my wife and my daughter—and our God . . . It's nobody's business but ours. Even presidents have private lives."[13]

Over the next few weeks, Clinton apologized publicly a few more times. He attended church and prayer meetings, asking for forgiveness. Each time, he was criticized by his enemies for being insincere. Then on September 9, Kenneth Starr released a detailed report of the results of his lengthy investigation into the Lewinsky matter. In his voluminous 445-page report, Starr accused Clinton of eleven offenses, which Starr's supporters stated could lead to impeachment. These crimes included perjury, obstruction of justice, and abuse of power.

The report also included graphic details of the president's affair with Lewinsky. The Republican-controlled House of Representatives released the report on the Internet, and a few days later televised some of Clinton's videotaped testimony before the grand jury. Polls showed that the majority of Americans thought that these tactics were unfair.

One reason Americans may have been so upset by the public release of the *Starr Report* was that until recent years, politicians' personal lives were never seen as public issues. Americans were not used to reading such private details about officeholders' lives, especially while the officials were still living. Presidents Franklin Roosevelt and John F. Kennedy both had extramarital affairs, but these were not reported until years after their deaths. Even Roosevelt's confinement to a wheelchair, due to the crippling effects of polio, was kept from the nation. Human weaknesses were thought to be inappropriate for the public's knowledge. Today there is a different understanding. If a president were confined to a wheelchair today, it would be impossible to conceal that fact. Why?

Some critics blame the Watergate scandal for providing the public with an excuse to know everything about their leaders. Other critics blame the sheer size and competitive nature of the corps of media members. Today there are many more reporters than there were in the days when Roosevelt and Kennedy held office.

In the case involving Clinton's inappropriate behavior, many American people were becoming as fed up with the media who were reporting the news as they were with the politicians who were making the news.

Meanwhile, Hillary Rodham Clinton defended her husband, and the two made appearances together in public. Nobody but Hillary Rodham Clinton could have known what she was thinking privately, but publicly she seemed devoted to her husband. Many Americans credited her with showing strength through a difficult time.

CNNenEspañol
Check out our
Spanish Specials

WARNING: The Mining Co.'s 500 Expert Guides will give you a whole new view of the Web. Since **The Mining Co.** is made up of **real people** who mine the Net so YOU DON'T HAVE TO, studies have shown that **The Mining Co.** can be highly habit forming. If you click here, you may never go back to using a search engine again.

interactive
CNN.com

allpolitics.com > storypage   TIME | CQ

MAIN PAGE
WORLD
U.S.
U.S. LOCAL
ALLPOLITICS
 TIME
 CQ
 analysis
 community
WEATHER
BUSINESS
SPORTS
SCI-TECH
ENTERTAINMENT
BOOKS
TRAVEL
FOOD
HEALTH
STYLE
IN-DEPTH

 custom news
 Headline News brief
 daily almanac
 CNN networks
 on-air transcripts
 news quiz

allpolitics
EN ESPAÑOL
em **português**
SVENSKA
NORGE

GO TO ...

 video on demand
 video archive
 audio on demand
 news email services
 free email accounts
 desktop headlines

Note: Some of the material in this report contains graphic descriptions of sexual encounters.

The content of the following materials are verbatim as forwarded by the Office of the Independent Counsel. The conversion to HTML has altered the pagination and format. The original Table of Contents is not provided.

Supporting Documents:
Documents released 9/21/98
Documents released 10/2/98
INTERACTIVE:
Our interactive guide allows you to browse the Starr Report by Table of Contents, Key Dates, or Names. You'll also find links to CNN background information, news stories, and related documents throughout.

Launch the interactive guide here or continue reading below.

Table of Contents

Chronology

Table of Names

The Principals
The First Family
Presidential Aides/Advisors/Assistants
Other White House Personnel
Department of Defense Employees

The Starr Report was released to the public on the Internet, as well as in book form.

In the wake of the *Starr Report,* some Clinton supporters decided the time was right to use the same unfair tactics people like David Brock had been using against Clinton for years. They leaked to the press information about three conservative Republicans who had also had illicit extramarital affairs: Indiana representative Dan Burton, Idaho representative Helen Chenoweth, and Illinois representative Henry Hyde. Hyde was also the chairman of the House Judiciary Committee and would oversee any impeachment hearing on the president's conduct that might result from Starr's investigation. Now all three congresspeople had to admit they, too, had been unfaithful to their spouses. Because they had criticized Clinton's lack of morals so strongly, each seemed hypocritical.

Although the American people were sick of the whole affair, on October 8 the House of Representatives voted 258 to 176 to open an impeachment inquiry against Clinton. The votes were mostly along party lines, although thirty-one Democrats voted with the Republicans.[14]

The main question was whether or not President Clinton's actions were serious enough to require impeachment, the first step in a two-step process that is required to remove an American president from office: First, the House of Representatives must vote on whether or not to officially impeach the president, or charge him with an official offense. If such a charge is approved by the House, then a second procedure, a trial, must take place before the United States Senate. The Senate acts as a jury. If two thirds of the Senators vote to convict the president of any charge, then the president is removed from office.

This process dates back to the nation's earliest days

and was provided for in the United States Constitution, which reads, "The President, Vice President and all civil Officers of the United States, shall be removed from Office on Impeachment for, and Conviction of, Treason, Bribery, or other high Crimes and Misdemeanors."

The president was not being accused of treason or bribery. However, if Clinton had committed perjury by lying under oath about his affair with Monica Lewinsky, did that act fall into the category of high crimes and misdemeanors as described by the Founding Fathers? Now it would be up to the House of Representatives to make that decision.

Amidst all the talk of scandal and impeachment came the 1998 congressional elections. All the members of the House of Representatives and thirty-three senators were up for reelection. Before the scandal broke, the Republicans had been expected to gain several seats in both houses of Congress. However, in November, when the election votes had been totaled, although the Republicans had held their number in the Senate, they had lost five seats in the House. Two Republican senators who were voted out of office were strong Clinton critics: Al D'Amato of New York and Lauch Faircloth of North Carolina. Democrats claimed that the votes conclusively showed that the public was against impeachment, but Republicans insisted polls had shown that the people had voted on other issues, unrelated to impeachment.

There were two other major casualties in the wake of the 1998 elections. Speaker of the House Newt Gingrich took the blame for the Republicans' disappointing showing in the elections and resigned his party's leadership. Representative Bob Livingston of Louisiana was chosen to replace him. However, before Livingston had a chance to become Speaker, it was leaked to the press that he, too, had had an extramarital affair years earlier. Following this disclosure, Livingston resigned his upcoming office. Ironically, Bill Clinton was still standing tall with high approval ratings from the American people.

Then, after four years of fighting Paula Jones's sexual harassment charges, Clinton's lawyers finally worked out an out-of-court settlement to pay Jones $850,000 to drop the case.[15] Clinton admitted no wrongdoing, nor did he apologize to Jones. To Clinton, it was a matter of getting the case behind him.

In Congress, neither the public's repudiation of the Republicans at the election, nor Clinton's increasingly high public approval ratings could stop the Republican-led impeachment crusade. On December 19, the House of Representatives voted to impeach Bill Clinton on two charges: perjury before a grand jury and obstruction of justice. The vote was almost entirely along party lines. The count of perjury was approved by a count of 228 to 206. A total of 223 Republicans voted for approval; 200 Democrats voted against it. The obstruction of justice article was approved, 221 to 212, with 216 Republicans in favor and 199 Democrats voting against it.[16]

The majority of Americans and members of the press attacked the impeachment vote. Most felt Clinton should have been censured, or officially criticized, for his actions but that removing him from office was going too far.[17]

On January 19, 1999, just hours before he was due to deliver one of the rosiest State of the Union addresses in the nation's history, the trial of President William Jefferson Clinton began in the United States Senate.

The Senate trial lasted for five weeks. Then on February 12, the birthday of Abraham Lincoln, the senators voted on whether Clinton was guilty of either or both charges. On the count of perjury, the vote was 55 not guilty, 45 guilty. The 55 not-guilty votes were from every Democratic senator and 10 Republicans. On the count of obstruction of justice, the vote was 50 guilty, 50 not guilty. A total of 5 Republicans joined the Democrats in voting not guilty on that count. As had been suspected all along, the two-thirds majority needed to convict the president on either count was not to be.

One year and one month after the Lewinsky matter had exploded onto the front pages of newspapers across the world, the president made a brief public statement on the White House grounds. He said,

> I want to say again to the American people how profoundly sorry I am for what I said and did to trigger these events and the great burden they have imposed on the Congress and on the American people. . . .This can be and this must be a time of reconciliation and renewal for America.[18]

As Clinton walked a few steps away from the podium towards the White House, a reporter called out, "In your heart, sir, can you forgive and forget?"

Clinton returned to the podium and announced, "I believe any person who asks for forgiveness has to be prepared to give it."[19]

Then he turned and entered the White House to finish his second term.

11

LEGACY

I t takes years for a president's legacy to be established. When presidents Harry S. Truman and Dwight D. Eisenhower left office, they were thought to be, at worst, poor presidents. At best, they were considered average. Yet historians today rank both past leaders as near great presidents.[1]

President Bill Clinton's legacy will take years to form. His former chief of staff, Leon Panetta, predicted that Clinton's lasting impact will, in the end, be about money. Panetta admitted, "A lot depends, but what he did on the deficit issue will have the most impact on the American people—that, and the fact that he was willing to take on trade issues."[2]

The numerous scandals, including the permanent stain of impeachment on Bill Clinton's record, are inescapable.

However, only time will tell whether history will show Clinton as a morally deficient leader or the victim of a witch-hunt conducted by his opponents.

What is certain is this—William Jefferson Clinton was the first baby boomer to be president, a king of comeback, and a political survivor. The changing tides of history cannot alter those facts.

SOURCE DOCUMENT

This cartoon, printed in The Buffalo News, *speculates on the future legacy of President Clinton, all the while poking fun at Clinton's ability to use language to manipulate the truth.*

Chronology

1946—Born in Hope, Arkansas, on August 19.

1953—Moved with family to Hot Springs, Arkansas.

1963—Met President Kennedy in a White House Rose Garden ceremony.

1964—Graduated from Hot Springs High School; enrolled at Georgetown University.

1966—Worked for Senator William Fulbright of Arkansas.
–1967

1968—Attended Oxford University in England as a Rhodes
–1970   Scholar.

1970—Attended Yale University Law School.
–1973

1973—Graduated from Yale Law School; accepted a teaching position at the University of Arkansas Law School.

1974—Lost election for House of Representatives.

1975—Married Hillary Rodham on October 11.

1976—Elected Arkansas attorney general.

1978—Elected governor of Arkansas.

1980—Daughter Chelsea born February 27; lost election for second term as governor.

1982—Won election to four more terms as governor.
–1990

1992—Elected president of the United States.

1993—Signed several laws, including Brady Law and NAFTA; health care reform plan introduced; United

States troops withdrawn from Somalia, sent to Macedonia; presided over peace ceremony between Israel and the Palestinians; Whitewater scandal emerged.

1994—Paula Jones case surfaced; health care reform failed; crime law, including partial assault weapons ban passed; GATT passed; United States sent troops to Haiti; Republicans swept midterm elections.

1995—Oklahoma City bombing, April 19; confirmation of affirmative action; Bosnia peace agreement and United States troops to Bosnia; two government shutdowns.

1996—Senate Whitewater hearings; financial partners found guilty of fraud in Whitewater case; welfare reform law passed; defeated Bob Dole to win second term as president; campaign fund-raising scandal.

1997—Senate campaign finance hearings; balanced-budget deal finalized; attacked tobacco industry; increased number of government scholarships for college students.

1998—Sixth straight year of economic prosperity; Monica Lewinsky scandal surfaced; Paula Jones case dropped, appealed, and finally settled; signed peace agreement in Ireland; House of Representatives voted to impeach Clinton.

1999—Acquitted on impeachment charges, February 12.

Chapter Notes

Chapter 1. A Strange Day in History

1. Federal News Service, "1998 State of the Union Address," as published on *The Washington Post* Internet site, www.washingtonpost.com, 1999.

2. Gary Fields, "Murder Rate Declines to 30-Year Low," *USA Today*, November 23, 1998, p. 1A.

3. Beth Belton and Rich Miller, "Good Times Are Here, but Just How Good?" *USA Today*, November 25, 1998, p. 3B.

4. Associated Press, "Poll: Public Disengaged from Trial," *MSNBC* Internet site, www.msnbc.com/news, January 18, 1999.

5. Ibid.

Chapter 2. A Place Called Hope

1. Personal interview with Joe Purvis, February 10, 1998.

2. David Maraniss, *First in His Class: A Biography of Bill Clinton* (New York: Simon & Schuster, 1995), p. 31.

3. Personal interview with David Leopoulos, February 9, 1998.

4. Ibid.

5. Ibid.

6. Howard Fineman and Ann McDaniel, "You Didn't Reveal Your Pain," *Newsweek*, March 30, 1992, p. 37.

7. Personal interview with Carolyn Staley, February 11, 1998.

8. Maraniss, p. 44.

9. Personal interview with Carolyn Staley, February 11, 1998.

10. Personal interview with David Leopoulos, February 9, 1998.

11. Maraniss, p. 48.

Chapter 3. Dominoes and Lotteries

1. Personal interview with Tom Campbell, March 14, 1998.

2. Ibid.

3. David Maraniss, *First in His Class: A Biography of Bill Clinton* (New York: Simon & Schuster, 1995), pp. 59–60.

4. Personal interview with Tom Campbell, March 14, 1998.

5. Maraniss, p. 90.

6. Jim Moore, *Young Man in a Hurry* (Fort Worth, Tex.: The Summit Group, 1992), pp. 31–33.

7. Personal interview with Dave Matter, March 17, 1998.

8. Ibid.

9. Personal interview with Carolyn Staley, April 3, 1998.

10. Matthew D'Ancona, "Dons Glory in Their Boy as Leader of Western World," *The London Times*, November 4, 1992, p. 3.

11. Ibid.

12. Roger Morris, *Partners in Power: The Clintons and Their America* (New York: Henry Holt and Company, 1996), p. 90.

Chapter 4. Love and Politics

1. Virginia Kelley with James Morgan, *Leading With My Heart* (New York: Simon & Schuster, 1994), p. 174.

2. Martin Walker, *The President We Deserve* (New York: Crown Publishers, Inc., 1996), p. 69.

3. Carl Sferrazza Anthony, "Clio and the Clintons," *American Heritage*, December 1994, p. 124.

4. Ibid.

5. Roger Morris, *Partners in Power: The Clintons and Their America* (New York: Henry Holt and Company, 1996), p. 165.

6. Ibid., p. 166.

7. Martha Sherrill, "The Rising Lawyer's Detour to Arkansas," *Washington Post*, January 12, 1993, p. B1.

8. Eleanor Clift, "'I Think We're Ready': Hillary Clinton Speaks out about Her Family, Her Career and Her Marriage," *Newsweek*, February 3, 1992, p. 21.

9. David Maraniss, *First in His Class: A Biography of Bill Clinton* (New York: Simon & Schuster, 1995), p. 337.

10. Ibid.

11. Personal interview with Joe Purvis, April 27, 1998.

12. Ibid.

13. Maraniss, p. 357.

Chapter 5. "An IQ of a Zillion"

1. Roger Morris, *Partners in Power: The Clintons and Their America* (New York: Henry Holt and Company, 1996), p. 219.

2. Personal interview with Rose Crane, April 16, 1998.

3. David Maraniss, *First in His Class: A Biography of Bill Clinton* (New York: Simon & Schuster, 1995), p. 379.

4. Personal interview with Rose Crane, April 16, 1998.

5. Maraniss, pp. 387–388.

6. Matthew Cooper, "How the Lessons of His 1980 Defeat Shape this Campaign," *U.S. News & World Report*, July 20, 1992, p. 33.

7. Personal interview with Elaine Johnson, April 16, 1998.

8. Ibid.

9. Ibid.

10. Martin Walker, *The President We Deserve* (New York: Crown Publishers, Inc., 1996), p. 98.

11. Personal interview with Paul Root, April 20, 1998.

12. Ibid.

13. Ibid.

14. Walker, p. 101.

15. Personal interview with Paul Root, April 20, 1998.

16. Walker, p. 102.

17. Maraniss, p. 421.

18. Personal interview with Mary Anne Salmon, April 20, 1998.

Chapter 6. "He Doesn't Quit."

1. Personal interview with Elaine Johnson, April 16, 1998.

2. DRI McGraw Hill Gallup Poll chart, "Slow Growth, Poor Rating," *The Boston Globe*, November 4, 1992, p. 27.

3. Martin Fletcher, "Comeback Kid Who Never Gave Up," *The London Times*, November 4, 1992, p. 2.

4. Personal interview with David Leopoulos, April 29, 1998.

5. Ibid.

6. Martin Walker, *The President We Deserve* (New York: Crown Publishers, Inc., 1996), p. 126.

7. Bill Nichols, "How Clinton Won," *USA Today*, November 4, 1992, p. 5A.

8. *The World Almanac and Book of Facts* (Mahwah, N.J.: World Almanac Books, 1997), p. 478.

9. Walker, p. 158.

Chapter 7. A Rough Start

1. Live coverage of Clinton inaugural, January 20, 1993, WCVB, Channel 7, Boston.

2. Ibid.

3. Martin Walker, *The President We Deserve* (New York: Crown Publishers, Inc., 1996), p. 172.

4. "7-Week Standoff: How It Happened," *USA Today*, April 20, 1993, p. 4A.

5. Elizabeth Drew, *On the Edge: The Clinton Presidency* (New York: Simon & Schuster, 1994), p. 131.

6. Michael Putzel, "Clinton Blames Koresh, Orders Probe of Siege," *The Boston Globe*, April 21, 1993, p. 1.

7. Drew, p. 24.

8. Live coverage of Mideast peace signing, September 13, 1993, NBC.

9. Drew, p. 161.

Chapter 8. The Fall and Rise of Bill Clinton

1. Personal interview with Leon Panetta, May 13, 1998.

2. Editors of *Time* magazine, *Time Annual 1994: The Year in Review* (New York: Time Books, 1994), p. 64.

3. Personal interview with Leon Panetta, May 13, 1998.

4. Ibid.

5. Martin Walker, *The President We Deserve* (New York: Crown Publishers, Inc., 1996), p. 338.

6. Editors of *Time* magazine, *Time Annual 1995: The Year in Review* (New York: Time Books, 1995), p. 42.

7. Lars-Erik Nelson, "Crisis Reveals Newt Depths of Pettiness," *New York Daily News*, November 16, 1995, p. 6.

8. Ibid; Susan Page, "How Clinton Won . . . and Dole Lost," *USA Today*, November 6, 1996, p. 19A.

9. *New York Daily News*, November 16, 1995, p. 1.

10. Page, p. 19A.

Chapter 9. Feeling Good at Election Time

1. Personal interview with Leon Panetta, May 13, 1998.

2. *The World Almanac and Book of Facts* (Mahwah, N.J.: World Almanac Books, 1997), p. 38.

3. Ibid.

4. Andrea Stone, "In Arlington Burial Flap, No Dirt Unearthed," *USA Today*, November 26, 1997, p. 11A.

5. Ibid.

Chapter 10. Impeachment

1. Doyle McManus, *Los Angeles Times*, as reported in *The Keene Sentinel*, "Even Starr's Allies are Dismayed by His Tactics," March 1, 1998, p. 1.

2. Ibid.

3. Francis X. Clines, "Paula Jones Case Is Dismissed; Judge Says Even If Tale Is True, Incident Was Not Harassment." *The New York Times*, April 2, 1998. p. 1.

4. Tom Curry, "Impeachment 1998, the Damage Done," *MSNBC* home page, www.msnbc.com/news, 1999.

5. *USA Today* online edition, "Clinton's Popularity Rises Despite Scandals," www.usatoday.com, April 10, 1998.

6. *MSNBC* online news, "Clinton Gets Low Marks on Character," March 5, 1998.

7. Ibid.

8. Laura Meckler, "From Welfare to Work," *Associated Press*, as printed in *The Keene Sentinel*, May 26, 1998, p. 1.

9. David Brock, "Letter to the President: The Fire This Time," *Esquire*, April 1998, p. 60.

10. Ibid., p. 62

11. Michelle Kibiger, "Study: Checks Stopped Gun Purchases," *USA Today*, June 22, 1998, p. 3A.

12. Bronwen Maddox, "3 AM: Clinton Tells America of His Regrets," *London Times* Internet site, www.sunday-times.cu/uk, August 18, 1998.

13. Ibid.

14. Reuters News Service, as published on ABC News World Internet site, abcnews.go/com, January 27, 1999.

15. CNN Interactive Internet site, "Jones v. Clinton Finally Settled," cnn.com/ALLPOLITICS/November 13, 1998.

16. CNN Interactive Internet site, "Newspapers Slam Everybody over Clinton Impeachment," December 20, 1998.

17. CNN Interactive Internet site, "Poll: Americans Remain Opposed to Impeachment," December 18, 1998; and CNN Interactive, "Newspapers Slam Everybody over Clinton Impeachment," December 20, 1998.

18. CNN Headline News cable channel, telecast February 12, 1999.

19. Ibid.

Chapter 11. Legacy

1. Robert K. Murray and Tim H. Blessing, "The Presidential Performance Study: A Progress Report," *The Journal of American History*, December 1983, p. 541; and William J. Ridings, Jr., and Stuart B. McIver, *Rating the Presidents: A Ranking of U.S. Leaders, From the Great and Honorable to the Dishonest and Incompetent* (Secaucus, N.J.: Citadel Press, 1997), p. 207.

2. Personal interview with Leon Panetta, May 13, 1998.

Further Reading

Cwiklik, Robert. *Bill Clinton: President of the 90s.* Brookfield, Conn.: Millbrook Press, 1997.

Healey, Tim. *The 1960's.* New York: Franklin Watts, 1988.

Heinrichs, Ann. *America the Beautiful: Arkansas.* Chicago: Children's Press, 1989.

Kelly, Michael. *Bill Clinton.* New York: Chelsea House, 1998.

Kent, Deborah. *The Vietnam War: "What Are We Fighting For?"* Springfield, N.J.: Enslow Publishers, Inc., 1994.

Landau, Elaine. *Bill Clinton: And His Presidency.* New York: Franklin Watts, 1997.

Myers, Walter Dean. *A Place Called Heartbreak: A Story of Vietnam.* Austin, Texas: Raintree Steck-Vaughn Publishers, 1993.

Stacey, T. J. *Hillary Rodham Clinton: Activist First Lady.* Springfield, N.J.: Enslow Publishers, Inc., 1994.

Places to Visit

Arkansas

Bill Clinton's boyhood home, Hope. (870) 777-4455. Tours are given through the six-room home where young Bill Clinton lived until age four. A visitor center next door has computer interactive and other exhibits on Clinton's years in Hope. Open year-round.

Connecticut

Museum of American Political Life, West Hartford. (860) 768-4090. The history of every presidential campaign in the United States is told through buttons, banners, photos, and videotape. Open year-round.

Massachusetts

The Museum at the John Fitzgerald Kennedy Library, Boston. (617) 929-4523. One of the dozens of exhibits showcases the 1963 meeting of Clinton and Kennedy. Open year-round.

Texas

George Bush Presidential Library and Museum, College Station. (409) 260-9552. The presidential library of Clinton's predecessor has a small exhibit devoted to the 1992 campaign. Open year-round.

Washington, D.C.

The White House. (202) 456-7041. Several rooms are open to visitors on certain weekday mornings. You can get tickets when you arrive or in advance through your senator or congressperson. Open year-round.

Internet Addresses

The Clinton boyhood home
<http://www.clintonbirthplace.com/>

George Bush Presidential Library and Museum
<http://www.csdl.tamu.edu/bushlib>

Information on all United States Presidents
<http://sunsite.unc.edu/lia/president/>

John F. Kennedy Library Foundation
<http://www.cs.umb.edu/jfklibrary/index.htm>

The National Park Service, including many presidential historic sites
<http://www.nps.gov>

The Richard Nixon Library and Birthplace
<http://www.chapman.edu/nixon>

The White House
< http://www.whitehouse.gov/>

White House Historical Association
<http://www.whitehousehistory.org>

Index